# knit.101

the indispensable
self-help
guide to knitting
and crochet

# knit.101

the indispensable
self-help
guide to knitting
and crochet

sixth&spring  books

sixth&spring books
233 Spring Street
New York, New York, 10013

Vice President, Publisher
**Trisha Malcolm**

Editorial Director
**Elaine Silverstein**

Editor-in-Chief, Knit.1
**Adina Klein**

Art Director
**Chi Ling Moy**

Graphic Designers
**Marie Nguyen**
**Sheena T. Paul**

Book Division Manager
**Erica Smith**

Associate Editor
**Erin Walsh**

Yarn Editors
**Tanis Gray**
**Veronica Manno**

Instructions Editor
**Pat Harste**

Instructions Proofreader
**Rita Greenfeder**

Writer
**Daryl Brower**

Copy Editors
**Wendy R. Preston**
**Kristina Sigler**

Technical Illustrations
**Uli Mönch**

Production Manager
**David Joinnides**

President and Publisher,
Sixth&Spring Books
**Art Joinnides**

How-to Photography: Marcus Tullis
Instructional photographs feature Lion Brand Yarn: Lion Cotton in #148 Turquoise,
#146 Fuchsia, and #158 Banana, and Lion Suede in #146 Fuchsia.

1  3  5  7  9  10  8  6  4  2

Manufactured in China

Library of Congress Control Number: 2006924830
ISBN-10: 1-931543-96-8
ISBN-13: 978-1-931543-96-5

# Contents

**Welcome** to the wild and woolly world of knit and crochet. It's a world where spare time becomes special time and pieces of string have a life of their own.

If you are like me, the word "trendy" makes you a little queasy. If that's the case, you might also be a tad sickened when things are hailed as "hot," "hip," "in" or "cool." Over the past few years, knitting has been hailed as all of the above. Well, please, I'm begging you, don't let that be the reason you want to learn to knit.

Why? Because the thing about something being "in" is that it implies it will eventually be "out." And one thing you will discover as you start knitting and crocheting is that these arts never go out of style. What better way to express yourself than by wearing a one-of-a-kind creation made with your two cute little hands!

As you work your way though our handbook, you certainly will get the basics—the how-tos for every stitch you will need. And you'll also find plenty of patterns for fun, funky, functional pieces. But I also think that as you go, you will make a deeper connection to these crafts and the power of your own hands. I encourage those of you starting out to stick with it: find at least twenty minutes to practice every day for a week. And remember, nobody is perfect! Your first attempts probably won't get you on Project Runway, but keep at it and enjoy the ride.

Get those needles clicking!

Adina Klein

All you need to knit are needles and a few balls of yarn, but we really get into all the gear that goes with it. One of the advantages of knitting today is the availability of more cool little gadgets and great-looking accessories for sale than you can shake a rosewood needle at. And, like most crafty types, we can't resist the lure of something that combines form and function in one perfect package. That said, we should point out that you don't need rhinestone-studded ebony needles and a totally rad knitting bag to start stitching—it's just that having them does make it that much more fun. In this chapter, you'll find what you really need to get knitting—feel free to add to the list by splurging on what you really want.

# Needles

Needles are obviously essential, since without them you won't be doing much knitting. There are several styles out there, all of which come in a wide variety of materials: aluminum, bamboo, even exotic woods like ebony and rosewood. Some are strictly functional; others double as art pieces in their own right. Which to use depends on your project and preference; try out a few different styles until you find one that works for you.

## Straight up

**Straight needles** are the long, straight (duh!) sticks that most of us associate with knitting. They have a point on one end and a knob on the other that keeps your stitches from sliding off the needle. (Once upon a time this was just a boring button, but these days it's likely to be anything from a cute polymer clay sculpture to a rhinestone-studded topper.)

Straights are sold in pairs of various lengths, with 10" and 14" being the most common, and they'll get you through the majority of the projects you encounter.

## Round about

**Circular needles** are shorter pointed sticks attached to one another with a length of smooth nylon cord. You can use them to knit

tubular pieces (leg warmers, hats, seamless sweaters) or flat pieces. If you do a lot of stitching on public transit or in crowded movie theaters, these are worth investigating. Since there's essentially no "end" to the needle, you won't poke the person seated next to you.

## Double time

**Double pointed needles (dpns)** have points on both ends and are used to make small items in the round, turn sock heels, or make I-cords. **Cable needles** are double points with a U shape in the center. As you've probably guessed, they're used in cable knitting (more on that in Chapter 6).

# String Theory

Can't do much knitting without yarn, can you? (Well, okay, you can use string or shredded T-shirts and plastic bags, but that's another book in itself. Let's stick to the basics here, shall we?) The fiber choices out there are pretty staggering and a whole lot of fun to explore. Let's start with your traditional **worsteds**. These smooth yarns are the classic choice for sweaters; they make stitch patterns stand out and are generally the easiest for beginners to work with. Then there are the **fuzzy, textured yarns** like angora, mohair, bouclé (which looks like little curlicues) and chenille. You'll find them in all-natural wool, cashmere, cotton, alpaca and other animal or plant fibers; acrylic and nylon; or blends of two or more (a little wool, a little acrylic; some alpaca mixed with silk—you get the idea). These give lots of romantic texture, but can be a bit trickier to knit with since all that fuzz makes it harder to see your stitches. **Ribbons and tapes** (which tend to turn up in nylon, cotton or silk) have a flat surface that makes for a more drapey fabric. Next up are the

**novelties**, all those fun and fabulous fake fur, eyelash, twist and combination yarns that came out during the hot scarf trend a few years back. These are great for making something incredibly simple (a garter-stitch scarf, for instance) look totally special. We also like them for accents on collars and cuffs. Like the other fuzzies, they make it a bit tricky to see stitches, but they also hide a multitude of beginner mistakes.

No matter what the fiber content, all yarns are grouped into basic categories (fingering, sport, DK, worsted, bulky, etc.) designed to help you pick the right one for your project—and your needle size. Weight (really the thickness of the yarn) is the measure by which all yarns are judged, and the industry has come up with a nifty standardized list of symbols and terms to help you identify it. For the most part you'll use thinner yarns on smaller needles and thicker yarns on bigger needles. Check the ball band (the little label wrapped around your yarn) for the symbols and information on the next page.

# Standard Yarn Weight System

## Categories of yarn, gauge ranges, and recommended needle and hook sizes

| Yarn Weight Symbol & Category Names | 1 Super Fine | 2 Fine | 3 Light | 4 Medium | 5 Bulky | 6 Super Bulky |
|---|---|---|---|---|---|---|
| Type of Yarns in Category | Sock, Fingering, Baby | Sport, Baby | DK, Light Worsted | Worsted, Afghan, Aran | Chunky, Craft, Rug | Bulky, Roving |
| Knit Gauge Range* in Stockinette Stitch to 4 inches | 27–32 sts | 23–26 sts | 21–24 sts | 16–20 sts | 12–15 sts | 6–11 sts |
| Recommended Needle in Metric Size Range | 2.25–3.25 mm | 3.25–3.75 mm | 3.75–4.5 mm | 4.5–5.5 mm | 5.5–8 mm | 8 mm and larger |
| Recommended Needle U.S. Size Range | 1 to 3 | 3 to 5 | 5 to 7 | 7 to 9 | 9 to 11 | 11 and larger |
| Crochet Gauge* Ranges in Single Crochet to 4 inch | 21–32 sts | 16–20 sts | 12–17 sts | 11–14 sts | 8–11 sts | 5–9 sts |
| Recommended Hook in Metric Size Range | 2.25–3.5 mm | 3.5–4.5 mm | 4.5–5.5 mm | 5.5–6.5 mm | 6.5–9 mm | 9 mm and larger |
| Recommended Hook U.S. Size Range | B–1 to E–4 | E–4 to 7 | 7 to I–9 | I–9 to K–10½ | K–10½ to M–13 | M–13 and larger |

**\* GUIDELINES ONLY: The above reflect the most commonly used gauges and needle or hook sizes for specific yarn categories.**

This *Standards & Guidelines* booklet and downloadable symbol artwork are available at: **YarnStandards.com**

# Extra Credit

Beyond yarn and a good assortment of needles, you'll need a few other tools and accessories to get yourself going. Some are more essential than others; we've broken the list down into the must-haves (The A-list) and the nice-to-haves (B-listers), below:

## The A-list
### Scissors

Whether you stick to a strictly utilitarian pair or splurge on a more decorative design (we love the little gold ones that are shaped like storks), you'll need these to cut yarn, make fringe and snip off loose ends. Pick a small pair with a sharp point that allows you to get close to the work. If you'll be doing a lot of knitting on the go, get a sleeve that protects the point or slip the scissors into a little zippered pouch so they won't poke holes in your bag—or cut your fingers when you reach in to grab them.

### Yarn needles

Sometimes called tapestry needles, these have a blunt point and a wide eye (that's the little hole at the top of the needle) to accommodate thick yarn. You'll need these to sew seams and weave in ends. The metal and colorful plastic styles available work equally well.

### Tape measure

You can't get your project right unless you know what size it is, so a tape measure is essential. Your basic yellow dressmaker's tape will do just fine, but many cute retractable styles exist that make measuring a little more fun. Just be sure the tape is marked in both inches and centimeters and is made of fiberglass, since cloth tends to stretch.

### Ruler or stitch gauge
One or the other is essential for checking the

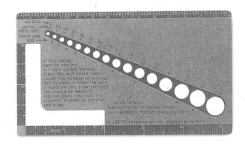

ever-important knitting gauge (more on that on pages 23–25). Rulers work just fine, but gauges have neat little windows that make it easier to count the number of stitches in a row. Some even have a row of holes you can use to identify the size of unmarked needles.

## Pins

Without these puppies, you'll have a hard time seaming and blocking. You'll want a good stock of long, straight pins with glass or metal heads (plastic will melt under the heat of your iron) and T-pins for blocking. You can also purchase special blocking pins that are longer and more flexible than traditional T-pins.

## Crochet hook

Every knitter needs at least one hook to help pick up stitches, make decorative edgings and seam slip stitches.

## Stitch holders

Slip open stitches (like those on a neckline) onto these oversized safety pins to keep them from unraveling until you are ready to pick them up again.

## Stitch markers

These little plastic or metal rings are handy for keeping track of things like where to increase and decrease or the beginning of a circular row. Split markers have a little slit in the ring so you can slip the marker into the stitches

## necessity is the mother of invention

Stuck short without the tool you need? Try these MacGyver-like substitutes:

**Stitch holder:** Thread stitches onto a length of fishing line or cording and tie the ends.

**Point protectors:** Push the needle tips into erasers or wrap rubber bands around the points.

**Cable needle:** A skinny pencil makes a nice substitute; just take care that yarn doesn't snag on the metal that holds the eraser.

**Stitch markers:** Tie short pieces of yarn into little loops and slip over your needles (a contrasting color will work best).

instead of over the needle. Lately, we've been seeing a lot of gorgeous ones trimmed with beads, crystals and other doodads. They don't work any better than the plain kind, but they'll make you feel like the glamorous girl who knits.

### Knitting tote

Is this an essential? Probably. You need a spot for storing your stuff, and while your old backpack or a plastic grocery sack will do the job just fine, it's kind of nice to have a beautiful bag to tote around town. Knitting bags have become an industry in their own right, so you'll have plenty to choose from. The best ones have multiple pockets for needles and accessories and offer easy access to your work-in-progress.

## B-Listers

These aren't essential, but they will make your knitting life easier:

### Pompom makers

These little plastic disks work like magic to create perfectly plush and perky pompoms. Follow the directions on the package to get the best results.

### Point protectors

These are little rubber thingies you put over the points of your needles to keep stitches from falling off. They also prevent needles from poking holes in your bag. They are available in lots of sizes, shapes and colors. We're partial to the little yellow ones shaped like socks.

### Bobbins

When you do colorwork, wind yarn around these little plastic holders, using them like small-scale balls of yarn. They help prevent tangles and make it easier to work the design.

### Needle cases

Like knitting bags, these little accessories have exploded in style and popularity. Some are simple plastic zippered cases, others are artfully designed rolls crafted from silk or other fab fabrics. Look for one with loops to hold hooks and needles and a flap or zippered closure to keep them from spilling out.

### Notebook

It's a good idea to keep a record of what you've made and how you did it. You can use a simple spiral-bound notebook to keep track of your progress, or splurge on one of the many knitting journals offering space to record everything from yarn and needle inventories to your thoughts on what you're knitting and why you're knitting it.

# here's how

Getting those first stitches on the needle is actually harder than knitting, but we'll get you through it. **Relax**, take a deep breath, and follow the pretty pictures.

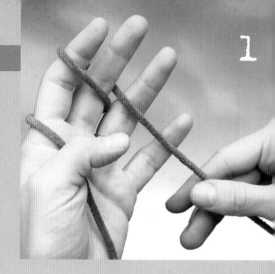

Okay, so you have your yarn, you have your needles and you're ready to start stitching— almost. Before you really get into the knitting groove, you have to create a foundation row for all those stitches. Doing this is called **"casting on,"** and it all starts with a little something called a **slip knot.**

This little loop is where it all begins. Channel your inner girl scout and let's get started....

## tip

If you're a newbie (or ever-so-slightly anal), you may cast on so tightly that when it comes time to knit you find it difficult to get the needle into the little loops. To loosen up, try casting on with a needle two sizes larger than the one you'll be using for the rest of the project. If on the other hand you're one of those slackers whose stitches come out loose and droopy, using a needle two sizes smaller should clean up your act.

# The

1. Hold the short end of the yarn in your palm and use your thumb to hold it in place. Wrap the yarn twice around the index and middle fingers.

2. Pull the strand attached to the ball through the loop between your two fingers, forming a new loop.

3. Place the new loop on the needle. Tighten the loop on the needle by pulling on both ends of the yarn to form the slip knot.

Knit Knack:

**1**

Knitting, you'll soon discover, is all about choices. And the cast-on, that foundation row from whence all stitches start, can be accomplished using several different methods. Which one you decide to use is mostly a matter of preference.

We're going to show you two of the most basic: the double cast-on (a.k.a. the long tail cast-on), which uses one needle and two lengths of yarn, and the knit-on cast-on, which uses two needles and one strand of yarn.

1. Make a slip knot on the right needle, leaving a long tail. Wind the tail end around your left thumb, front to back. Wrap the yarn from the ball over your left index finger and secure the ends in your palm.

2. With us so far? Good. Now insert the needle upward in the loop on your thumb.

3. Then with the needle, draw the yarn from the ball through the loop to form a stitch.

4. Take your thumb out of the loop and tighten the loop on the needle. Continue in this way until the correct number of stitches is cast on.

## double cast-on how to

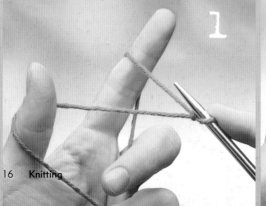

**1**

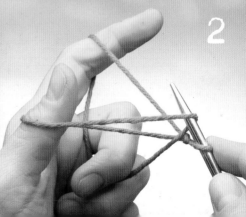

**2**

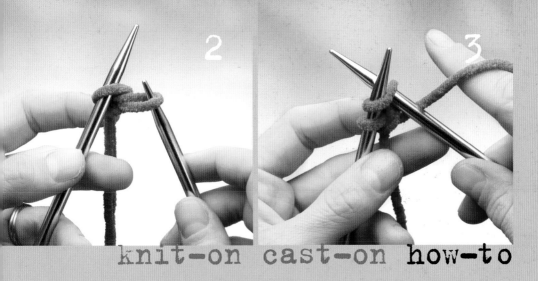

## knit-on cast-on how-to

1. Make a slip knot on the left needle. *Insert the right needle from front to back into the loop on the left needle.

2. Wrap the yarn around the right needle in a clockwise motion. Draw the yarn through the first stitch to make a new stitch, but don't drop the stitch from the left needle.

3. Slip the new stitch to left needle, just like the photo shows. Repeat from the * in Step 1 until the required number of stitches are cast on.

# Casting

That wasn't so bad, was it? Practice makes perfect (or at least builds confidence), so keep casting on until you feel comfortable with the technique and your stitches look reasonably neat and even.

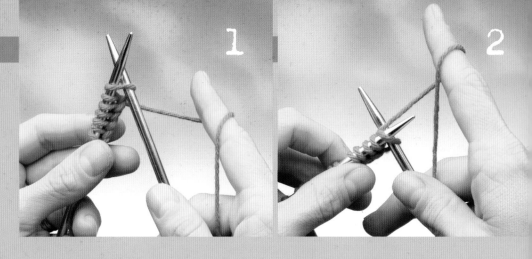

Got your **cast-on** down? Good. Now it's time for the fun stuff. You are ready to learn to knit. But first you have to decide if you'll be using the **English** or the **Continental** method. Both are **easy** to do and will achieve the same end result, so just pick the one that seems most comfortable. Here's how to get started:

1. Hold the needles as described in Step 1 of the English method (opposite), but hold the yarn with your left hand rather than your right. Insert the right needle from front to back into the first cast-on stitch on the left needle. Keep the right needle under the left, with the yarn in back of both needles.

2. Lay the yarn over the right needle as shown.

3. With the tip of the right needle, pull the strand through the cast-on stitch. Use your right index finger to hold the strand if you need to.

4. Slip the cast-on stitch off the left needle, leaving the newly formed stitch on the right needle. Repeat these steps until you've transferred all of the stitches from the left needle to the right. Got it? Good. You've just completed one row of stitching.

## continental method how to

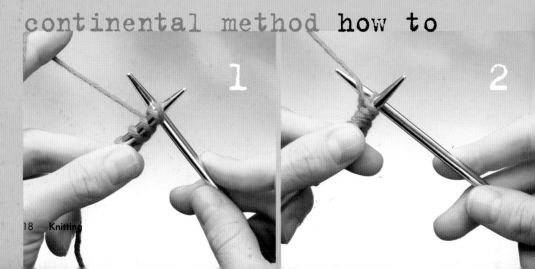

## the english method how-to

1. Hold the needle with the cast-on stitches in your left hand. Hold the empty needle in your right hand, and wrap the yarn tail around your index finger. Slip the right needle from front to back into the loop on the left needle. Keep the right needle under the left and the yarn at the back.

2. Wrap the yarn over and under the right needle in a clockwise motion.

3. With the right needle, catch the yarn and pull it through the cast-on stitch.

4. Slip the cast-on stitch off the left needle, leaving the newly formed stitch on the right needle. Repeat these steps in each subsequent stitch until all stitches are off the left needle. Ta-da! You've made one row of stitches.

# The Knit Stitch

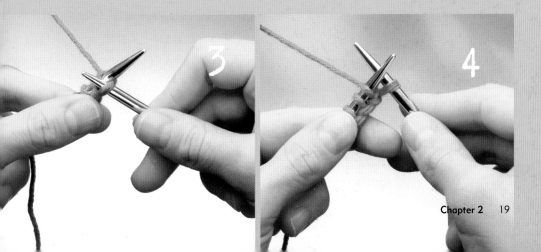

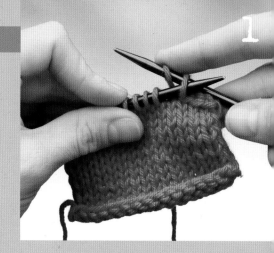

Your first row is **complete**, but one row does not a sweater, scarf or MP3 cozy make. If you want your stitches to shape up into something usable, you're going to have to **keep going**. Here's where

# The Garter Stitch

we introduce you to garter stitch, that most basic of all stitch patterns. All you do is knit **every row** and you'll end up with a flat, reversible ridged fabric that looks like this:

It's ultra-easy to do. Really. Here's how it works. When you get to the end of your first row of knit stitches, **just switch the needles** in your hands. Now the needle with the stitches on it is in your **left** hand and the empty needle is in your **right**. Start knitting each stitch again (following steps 1 to 4 of either the English or the Continental method as shown on the previous pages). It may look a little wonky at first, but after a few rows you'll have something that really resembles a strip of fabric. Pretty cool, huh?

## tip

The steps opposite show how a basic bind-off is done using stockinette stitch (explained on page 33). The swatch photographed may look a little different than yours, but trust us, the process is exactly the same for the garter stitches you've learned so far.

binding off how-to

# Off

At some point all good things must come to an end. Once your knitted fabric is the length you want it to be, you'll stop knitting and start binding off. (Unless, of course, you plan to trail around an unending afghan á la the Tita character in *Like Water for Chocolate*). Binding off gets the stitches off the needle and keeps them from unraveling all over the floor. So here we go:

**1. Knit two stitches. *Insert the left needle into the first stitch on the right needle.**

**2. Pull this stitch over the second stitch and off the right needle.**

**3. One stitch remains on the right needle (take a look at the picture). Knit the next stitch.**

Continue binding off by repeating from the * in step 1 until you have bound off all but one stitch. Carefully slip that stitch off the needle and pull the tail of the yarn through the loop. Remember to take it easy as you do this. Binding off too tightly (a common beginner's mistake) will make the edges pucker, something that won't add any beauty points to your work. If you find your bind-off is too tight, try using a needle a size or two larger than the one used in the project to loosen things up.

# Joining Yarn

So there you are, knitting up a blue streak, feeling pretty sure of yourself, when wham!— you're out of yarn. Don't panic, things are not at a crisis point. All you need to do is join a new ball of yarn. Try to do this at the end of a row, even if it means cutting off some of the yarn from the previous ball. It may seem like a waste, but it will make it easier to weave in the ends later and the stitches won't be distorted. Here's how:

## Joining yarn at the end of a row

Tie the yarn from the new ball loosely around the old, leaving a six-inch tail. Untie the knot later and weave the ends into the seam. If you must join a new ball mid-row, use this method:

## Joining yarn mid-row

**1.** Insert the right needle into the next stitch to be worked, wrap the new yarn around the right needle and start knitting with the new yarn.

**2.** Work to the end of the row. Tie the old and new strands together loosely before continuing so they will not unravel.

# Follow the Instructions

Remember that test they used to give in grade school? The one with a list of 20 items, beginning with: "1. Read through all the instructions below." Then you'd go on to answer all kinds of crazy questions, only to reach number 20, which read: "Do not answer any of the questions above." Think of knitting instructions the same way. Read through the entire pattern before you cast on a single stitch. Circle or highlight the information that pertains to your size and look up any unfamiliar terms or abbreviations before you start (the glossary on pages 114-115 is a great reference). Plan ahead and you won't come across any surprises to upset your knitting groove.

# Size Matters

Knit.1 patterns (and most others) provide instructions for the smallest size, with larger sizes given in parentheses: S (M, L), for example. So if the pattern says to cast on: 43 (44, 46) stitches, that means you would cast on 43 stitches for a size Small, 44 stitches for a size Medium and 46 stitches for a size Large. Highlighting or circling the numbers that pertain to your size will make it easier to follow the pattern. Get the complete scoop on sizing on page 96.

# Gauge

Knitting gauge—the number of rows and stitches per inch—determines the size of the garment (or bag, or blanket) you are making. It's also one of the most important factors in your knitting. Every pattern states the gauge on which the sizing for the project is based (in the U.K. they call it "tension"). If you don't get it right from the get-go, you risk ending up with a garment that doesn't fit. And since everything from the size and brand of the needles you're using to how loosely or tightly you knit can affect your gauge, you should always, always, always test your knitting against the pattern gauge before you begin the project. How do you do this? Simple. You make a gauge swatch. Basically this is just a square piece of knitted fabric that demonstrates how you, the needles and the yarn all work together. (Think of it as a trial run, or as Yarn Harlot Stephanie Pearl-McPhee likes to call it, a first date.) Start by gathering up the exact yarn and needles you intend to use for the project. Cast on enough stitches to create a square at least 4 inches wide—anywhere from 12–20 depending upon the size of the needles and the thickness of the yarn you are using should do it. Then knit or work in the specified stitch pattern until the square is a little more than 4 inches high.

Slip the stitches off the needle (no need to bind off unless you really want to) and put the swatch down on a table or other smooth, hard surface.

**1.** Use a tape measure or ruler to measure 4 inches across the swatch. Count the number of stitches in those 4 inches. This will give you the number of stitches.

**2.** Using the same ruler or tape, measure from the bottom to the top of the swatch and count the number of stitches in those 4 inches. This will give you the number of rows.

**3.** If you're a gadget geek, use a stitch gauge to get the same results. Place the gauge on your swatch and count the stitches that appear in the window.

Compare these numbers to those in the gauge given for your pattern. If they match, you are ready to get started. If they don't, you'll have to change your needle size and try again. If you were short a few stitches, try using smaller needles. If you had too many stitches, try using larger needles. (As a general rule, larger needles give fewer stitches to the inch, smaller needles give more.) Try different needle sizes until you get the correct gauge. We know it's a drag, but trust us: It's really worth your time. If your knitting is as much as a half an inch off from the recommended gauge, you can end up with a HUGE difference in the size of your

finished garment. (And that cute cropped cardi could end up with shoulders wide enough to fit your sister's linebacker boyfriend.) It's also a good idea to recheck your gauge once you have about 5 inches or so completed on the actual project.

For those of you still questioning the necessity of knitting a gauge swatch, take a gander at the pic opposite. Both swatches have exactly the same number of stitches and rows, but the one on the left was stitched with needles one size smaller than the one on the right. Now repeat after us: "I will knit a gauge swatch for every project I undertake, always and without exception."

# Abbreviations

At first glance, knitting instructions can look like some weird form of code: "Cast on 22 sts *K1, P2, rep from *." This can lead a · beginner to use some choice code of her own, as in: "What the @!#!& is that supposed to mean?" Don't freak. All those weird-looking strings of letters, numbers and symbols are part of a system of knitting terminology used to save space and make instructions easier to read. (No, really!) K1, for instance, simply means knit one stitch. Rep from * means to repeat the instructions after the asterisk as many times as indicated. Sts stands for stitches. You'll find a complete listing of abbreviations and terms on page 114 of this book.

Now the real fun begins. On the next few pages you'll find two ultra-easy designs you can get started on now.

## materials

9 balls in #402 of Wheat Wool-Ease Thick & Quick® by Lion Brand, 6oz/170g
balls, each approx 106 yd/97m (acrylic/wool)

One pair size 50 (25mm) needles (Speed Stix) OR SIZE TO OBTAIN GAUGE

## finished measurements

Approx 12"/30.5cm wide x 10'/3.05m long

## the gauge

4 sts and 5 rows to 4"/10cm with 3 strands held tog over garter st using size 50
(25mm) needles. BE SURE TO GET THE GAUGE.

## make the scarf

■ With 3 strands held tog, cast on 12 sts. Work in garter st (K every row) for 10
feet/3m or until desired length. Bind off loosely.

Simple garter stitch is all you need to create this cozy scarf. Knit one for your favorite guy in super-bulky yarn. You can do it!

This nifty messenger bag will double
as a carryall for your next knitting
project. Garter stitch and chunky
yarn will have it flying off your
needles in no time.

## materials

3 balls in #133 Pumpkin of Wool-Ease Thick & Quick® by Lion Brand, 6oz/170g balls, each approx 106yd/97m (acrylic/wool)

One pair size 13 (9mm) needles OR SIZE TO OBTAIN GAUGE

One 1"/25mm buckle

## finished measurements

Approx 12"/30.5cm wide, 9½"/24cm high and 3½"/9cm deep (excluding shoulder strap)

## the gauge

9 sts and 16 rows to 4"/10cm over garter st using size 13 (9mm) needles. BE SURE TO GET THE GAUGE.

## make the back/front flap

■ Cast on 30 sts. Work in garter st until piece measures 10"/25.5cm from beg. Mark beg and end of last row for end of back and beg of front flap. Cont to work until piece measures 20"/51cm from beg. Bind off all sts knitwise.

## make the front

■ Cast on 30 sts. Work in garter st until piece measures 10"/25.5cm from beg. Bind off all sts knitwise.

## make the sides/shoulder strap

■ Cast on 9 sts. Work in garter st until piece measures 58"/147cm from beg. Bind off all sts knitwise.

## make the buckle strap

■ Cast on 3 sts. Work in garter st for 4"/10cm. Bind off all sts knitwise.

## make the belt strap

■ Cast on 3 sts. Work in garter st for 6½"/16.5cm. Bind off all sts knitwise.

## finish the bag

■ Sew short ends of sides/shoulder strap tog. With WS facing, center seam of sides/shoulder strap along cast-on edge of back/front flap; pin pieces tog. Continue to pin sides/shoulder strap along side edges of back/front flap to markers.

■ Sew seam. On RS of front, center buckle strap along bottom edge, cast-on edges even. Pin edges tog, then pin entire strap to front to prevent it from getting caught up in stitching.

■ With WS facing, center seam of sides/shoulder strap along cast-on edge of front; pin pieces tog. Continue to pin sides/shoulder strap along side edges of front to bound-off edge.

■ Sew seam. Turn right side out. Unpin buckle strap. Make the belt loop. Cut 3 strands of yarn 20"/51cm long. Knot strands tog at one end. Braid strands tog, then knot ends. Wrap loop around buckle strap, then sew ends tog securely.

■ Attach buckle to end of strap. Tack down side edges of buckle strap, securing belt loop in center, and leaving top 1"/2.5cm below buckle unstitched.

■ Pin cast-on edge of belt strap 3½"/9cm from bound-off edge of front flap and centered side to side. Sew in place.

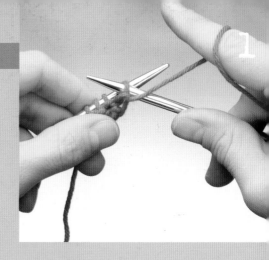

Garter stitch is great, but to really experience all of knitting's creative possibilities you need to take the next step and learn to purl. Purling is really just a backward version of knitting. Put the two together and you can create hundreds of different stitch patterns. (Kind of mind-blowing, isn't it?)

# The                    Stitch

Some people find purling a bit more awkward than knitting (that's why we showed you how to knit first), but with practice you should find it just as easy to do. As with the knit stitch, you can take your pick from two methods of purling: English and Continental, whichever you're most comfortable with.

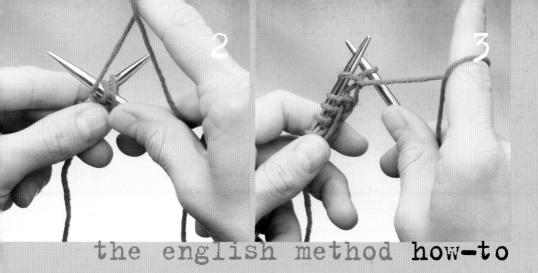

## the english method **how-to**

1. Hold the needle with the cast-on stitches in your left hand and the empty needle in your right (just as you did for knitting). This time, however, the tail of the yarn goes in front of the needle.

2. Insert the right needle from back to front into the first stitch on the left needle. The right needle is now in front of the left needle and the yarn is at the front of the work. With your right index finger, wrap the yarn counterclockwise around the right needle.

3. Draw the right needle and the yarn backward through the stitch on the left needle, forming a loop on the right needle.

4. Slip the stitch off the left needle. You have made one purl stitch. That wasn't so bad, was it? Repeat these steps until all of the stitches are off of the left needle. You've made one row of purl stitches.

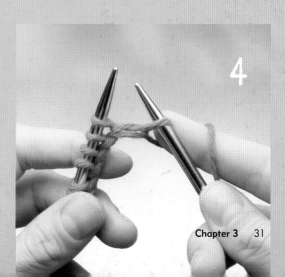

1. Hold the needle with the cast-on stitches in your left hand and the empty needle in your right (just as you did for knitting). This time, however, the tail of the yarn goes in front of the needle. Insert the right needle from back to front into the first stitch on the left needle, keeping the yarn in front of the needle.

2. Lay the yarn over the right needle as shown. Pull down on the yarn with your left index finger to keep it taut.

3. Bring the right needle and the yarn backward through the stitch on the left needle, forming a loop on right needle. (Still with us? Good.)

4. Slide the stitch off the left needle. Use your left index finger to tighten the new purl stitch on the right needle.

Continue to **repeat** these steps until you have worked all of the stitches from the left needle to the right needle. You have made one row of **purl stitches**. Congratulations! Go get a slice of chocolate cake or something.

## continental method how to

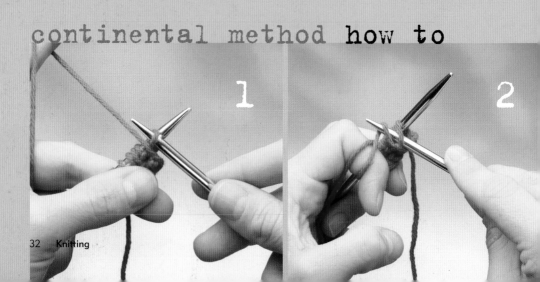

# Stockinette

Once you've learned how to knit and purl you can put the two together to form that **V-patterned fabric** most people associate with knitting: the **stockinette** stitch. How, you ask? Easy, we say. You simply knit one row, then purl the next, alternating every row until you have a piece of knitting that looks like this:

Lovely, isn't it? Now turn the page for a few **ideas** of what to do with it.

Now that you know how to knit and purl, practice both by alternating rows for these fun, funky sleeves. No need to sew them on—just button them to your T-shirt and go!

## materials

2 (3, 3) balls in #208 Copper Penny of Incredible by Lion Brand, 1¾oz/50g ball, approx 110yd/100m (nylon)

One pair size 15 (10mm) needles OR SIZE TO OBTAIN GAUGE

T-shirt with short cap sleeves

Twelve ¾"/19mm buttons

Sized for Small (Medium, Large). Shown in size Small

## finished measurements

Top of sleeve approx 8 (9¼, 10¾)"/20.5 (23.5, 27.5)cm around, unstretched.

## the gauge

12 sts and 12 rows to 4"/10cm, over St st using size 15 (10mm) needles. BE SURE TO GET THE GAUGE.

## make the sleeves

■ Starting at the top of sleeve, cast on 24 (28, 32) sts. Work in St st until piece measures desired length from edge of T-shirt sleeve to wrist (or 2½"/6.5cm less than total desired length). Work in garter st for 10 rows. Bind off. Sew sleeve seams.

## finish the T-shirt

■ Sew 6 buttons evenly spaced around edge of each T-shirt sleeve. Attach knitted sleeve to T-shirt by pulling buttons through sts at top of knitted sleeve.

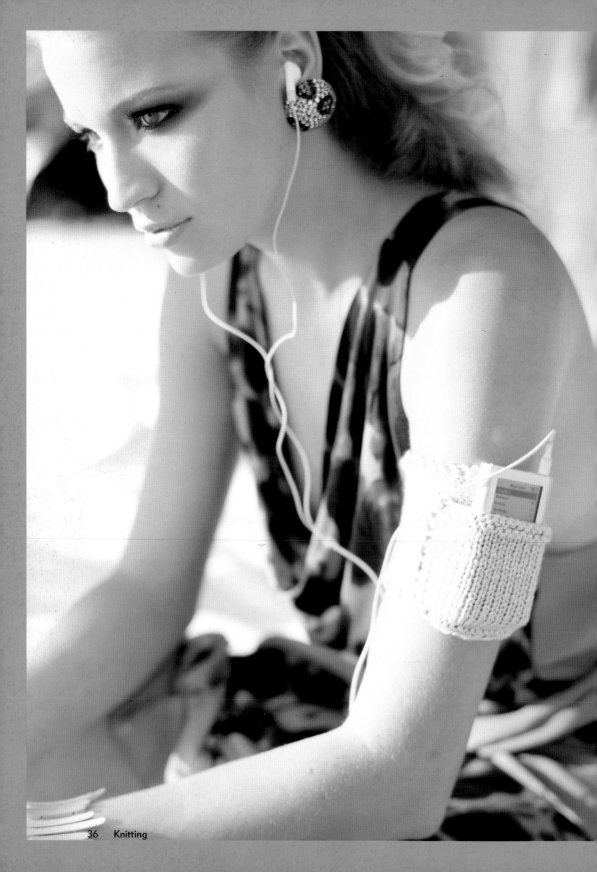

One way to show off your skill is with an accessory that you take everywhere. This armband, designed in easy stockinette stitch, holds keys, an MP3 player, cash—you name it!

## materials

1 ball in #170 Gold of Glitterspun by Lion Brand, 1¾oz/50g balls, each approx 115yd/105m (acrylic/cupro/polyester)
One pair size 7 (4.5mm) needles OR SIZE TO OBTAIN GAUGE
Velcro-brand Soft & Flexible Sew-on Tape

## finished measurements

Approx 8½"/21.5cm around by 4½"/11.5cm long

## the gauge

22 sts and 30 rows to 4"/10cm over St st using size 7 (4.5mm) needles. BE SURE TO GET THE GAUGE.

## make the armband

■ Cast on 24 sts. K 4 rows. **Next row (RS)** Knit. **Next row** K2, p20, k2. Rep last 2 rows until piece measures 8"/20.5cm, or ½"/1cm less than desired width, end with a RS row. K 4 rows. Bind off.

## make the pocket

■ Cast on 20 sts. K 2 rows. **Next row (RS)** Knit. **Next row** K2, p16, k2. Rep last 2 rows until piece measures 2¾"/7cm, end with a RS row. K 4 rows. Bind off.

## finish the armband

■ Cut the Velcro to fit along the cast-on edge of armband. Sew one side of Velcro to the WS of the bound-off edge and the other side of the Velcro to the RS of the cast-on edge.
■ Sew cast-on and two sides of pocket to center of armband.

When you're just getting started, practice makes perfect. This necklace scarf provides an opportunity to get into a relaxing rhythm.

## materials

2 balls in #194 Lime, #133 Tangerine, #132 Olive or #191 Violet of Fun Fur by Lion Brand, 1¾oz/50g balls, each approx 60yd/54m (polyester)

One pair size 10 (6mm) needles OR SIZE TO OBTAIN GAUGE

## finished measurements

Approx 4"/10cm (rolled) wide by 56"/142cm long

## the gauge

18 sts and 20 rows to 4"/10cm over St st using size 10 (6mm) needles.

BE SURE TO GET THE GAUGE.

## make the scarf

▦ Beg at one short end, cast on 22 sts.

▦ Work even in St st until ball is finished.

▦ Join 2nd ball of yarn and work in St st until ball is completed, leaving a few yards for binding off and seaming.

## finish the scarf

▦ Sew short ends tog to form "necklace."

This stylish shoulderette looks deceptively complicated, but is simple to knit and wear. Two garter-stitch chenille tubes are interlocked to form this plush wrap.

## materials

3 balls in #189 Wine of Chenille Thick & Quick® by Lion Brand, each ball approx 100yd/90m (acrylic/rayon)
One pair size 11 (8mm) needles OR SIZE TO OBTAIN GAUGE

## finished measurements

15"/38cm wide by 20"/51cm around

## the gauge

13 sts to 6"/15cm and 14 rows to 4"/10cm over garter st (slightly stretched) using size 11 (8mm) needles.
BE SURE TO GET THE GAUGE.

## make the shoulderette

▨ Beg at one short end, cast on 32 sts.
▨ Work in garter st until piece measures 20"/51cm from beg, stretching slightly.
▨ Bind off.
▨ Sew cast-on edge to bound-off edge (adjust length at this point, after tying on, if desired).

## make the band

▨ Cast on 7 sts. Work in garter st for 6"/15cm. Bind off.
▨ Looping the band over the seam at front, sew ends of band tog to form the ring closure.
▨ Tack the band in place, through the gathers of the shoulderette.

As we mentioned earlier, knit and purl stitches can be combined in many different ways to create all kinds of cool, textural patterns. To do this, switch back and forth between knit and purl stitches within the same row.

# Ribs and Other Textured Stitches

## Ribbing

This is one of the most widely used knit and purl combinations. Since the pattern is very stretchy, it's found most often on sweater hems, cuffs and necks. Used in the main body of a sweater, it creates a body-hugging fabric.

Ribbing is also incredibly easy to do. In the most basic form, you knit one stitch, purl the next and keep alternating until you reach the end of the row.

Easy, huh? The other great thing about ribbing is that once you've done a row or two, you can put down your instructions and let the stitches show you what to do. Knit the stitches that look like a "v" and purl the ones that look like a bump. The tricky part is remembering to move the yarn from back to front and front to back as you make the different knit and purl stitches. If you don't, you'll end up with extra stitches on the needle and a very lumpy-looking rectangle. Confused? Don't be. The pictures at right should make things clearer.

When knitting a stitch, the yarn is always held at the back of the work. When you purl, the yarn is held in the front. With us so far? When you are working the rib, remember to make sure that the yarn is in the correct position to work the next stitch.

For a knit 1, purl 1 rib, for example, you would knit the first stitch keeping the yarn to the back of the work. Before you purl the next stitch, slip the yarn between the needles (not over them!) and bring it to the front of the work.

**Yarn in back**          **Yarn in front**

## Seed stitch

This is another easy stitch that adds lots of great texture to your project. It starts out like a rib. For the first row (which will be the right side of your fabric), you'll follow a knit 1, purl 1 pattern across the row. But on the second row, you'll follow a purl 1, knit 1 pattern. In the end, you'll get a bumpy little surface that looks like example 1, opposite.

### 1. Seed stitch

(Over an even number of sts)

**Row 1 (RS)** *K1, p1; rep from * to end.

**Row 2** *P1, k1; rep from * to end.

Rep rows 1 and 2.

## Moss stitch

For this ultra easy stitch, simply alternate ribbed rows with rows that are knit straight across.

### 2. Moss stitch

(Multiple of 2 sts plus 1)

**Rows 1 and 3 (RS)** Knit.

**Row 2** P1, *k1; rep from * to end.

**Row 4** K1, *p1; k1; rep from * to end.

Rep rows 1–4.

## Basketweave

Let us now throw another simple knit and purl combination into your hands (you're ready for it, trust us). Basketweave combines knit and purl stitches to create a fabric that looks like—you guessed it—a woven basket (hence the name). We love it for scarves and pillows, but you can use it pretty much anywhere. Here's how it looks:

### 3. Basketweave

(Multiple of 8 sts plus 5)

**Row 1 (RS)** Knit.

**Row 2** K5, *p3, k5; rep from * to end.

**Row 3** P5, *k3, p5; rep from * to end.

**Row 4** Rep row 2.

**Row 5** Knit.

**Row 6** K1, *p3, k5; rep from *, end last rep k1.

**Row 7** P1, *k3, p5; rep from *, end last rep p1.

**Row 8** Rep row 6.

Rep row 1–8.

There are lots of variations to the stitches we've shown you here (k2, p2 ribs, double seed stitch, for example), plus a whole slew of other patterns. If you are interested in exploring the possibilities, get yourself a stitch dictionary, which provides pictures of many different stitches along with instructions for how to create them.

For now, let's see what we can do with the stitches you've learned so far. Here are a few quick projects....

The interplay of vertical ribs and horizontal stripes in these boot covers will keep your attention. Self-patterning yarn means no need to worry about joining new colors.

## materials

1 ball in #201 Denim Stripe of Magic Stripes by Lion Brand, 3½oz/100g ball, approx 330yd/300m (wool/nylon)

1 ball in #102 Ranch Red of Wool-Ease by Lion Brand, 3oz/85g ball, approx 197yd/180m (acrylic/wool)

One set (4) each sizes 2 and 3 (2.75 and 3.25mm) double pointed needles (dpns) OR SIZE TO OBTAIN GAUGE

Stitch marker

Purchased appliqué letters

Fabric glue

## finished measurements

Circumference (unstretched) 6"/15.2cm

Length 16¼"/42cm

## the gauge

40 sts and 32 rnds to 4"/10cm over k3, p2 rib (unstretched) using larger dpns. BE SURE TO GET THE GAUGE.

## make two boot covers

▓ Beg at lower edge with Ranch Red and larger size dpn, cast on 60 sts. Divide sts evenly onto 3 needles (20 sts on each needle). Join, being careful not to twist sts on needles. Place marker to mark beg of rnd. **Rnd 1** *K3, p2; rep from * around. **Rnds 2–7** Rep rnd 1. **Rnds 8–17** With Denim Stripe, work in k3, p2 rib. Change to smaller size dpn, cont in rib with Denim Stripe for 80 rnds more. Then, change to larger size dpn and cont in stripes as foll: 4 rnds Ranch Red, 8 rnds Denim Stripe, 6 rnds Ranch Red, 6 rnds Denim Stripe, 8 rnds Ranch Red. Bind off all sts loosely.

## make two straps

▓ With larger needle and Ranch Red, cast on 7 sts. Work in k1, p1 rib for 8"/20cm. Bind off.

## finish the boot covers

▓ Sew straps to ankle edge of boot covers, overlapping on the RS by ½"/1.5cm, or as necessary to fit. Glue "k1" appliqué to outside of each boot cover foll photo.

This ribbed scarf is a perfect backdrop for knit/purl combinations. The smooth yarn shows off your developing skills using easy-to-do patterning.

## materials

3 balls in #124 Camel of Lion Cashmere Blend by Lion Brand, 1.5oz/40g ball, each approx 84yd/71m (merino wool/nylon/cashmere)
One pair size 9 (5.5mm) knitting needles OR SIZE TO OBTAIN GAUGE
Stitch marker

## finished measurements

Width 5½"/14 cm
Length 48"/122 cm

## the gauge

17 sts and 22 rows to 4"/10cm over St st using size 9 (5.5 mm) needles. BE SURE TO GET THE GAUGE.

## make the scarf

■ Cast on 24 sts. **Row 1** *K1, p1; rep from* to end. **Row 2** *P1, k1; rep from * to end. **Row 3** K1, p1, k across to last st, p1. **Row 4** P1, k1, p across to last st, k1. **Rows 5–8** Rep rows 3 and 4 twice more. **Row 9** K1, p across to last 2 sts, k1, p1. **Row 10** P1, k across to last st 2 sts, p1, k1. **Rows 11–14** Rep rows 9 and 10 twice more. Rep rows 3–14 twice more. Rep rows 3–8. **Row 45** K1, p1, [p4, k4] twice, k5, p1. **Row 46** P1, k1, [k4, p4] twice, p5, k1. Rep last 2 rows 13 times more. Rep last 72 rows 3 times. Rep rows 3–44. Rep rows 1–2. Bind off all sts.

Take your sweet time with this crafty project. This knitted clock is dressed up with a seed-stitch border and antique buttons from stash (you have one, right?).

## materials

1 ball in #201 Denim Stripe of Magic Stripes by Lion Brand, 3½oz/100g ball, each approx 330yd/300m (wool/nylon)

One pair size 7 (4.5mm) needles OR SIZE TO OBTAIN GAUGE

Twelve assorted vintage buttons

One 10½"/26.5cm square piece of cardboard

All-purpose glue

Walnut Hollow Clock Crafts 3-piece kit

## finished measurements

10½"/26.5cm square

## the gauge

18 sts and 24 rows to 4"/10cm over St st using size 7 (4.5mm) needles and 2 strands of yarn. BE SURE TO GET THE GAUGE.

## seed-stitch pattern

Over an even number of sts:

**Row 1** *K1, p1; rep from * to end. **Row 2** K the purl and p the knit sts. Rep row 2 for seed st pat.

## make the clock

Cast on 50 sts with 2 strands of yarn. Work in seed st for 8 rows.

**Next row (RS)** Work 7 sts in seed st, k36, work 7 sts in seed st.

**Next row (WS)** Work 7 sts in seed st, p36, work 7 sts in seed st. Rep the last 2 rows until piece measures 9¾"/25cm from beg.

Work 7 rows in seed st on all sts. Bind off in pat.

## finish the clock

Block lightly to finished measurements.

Sew on buttons to mark the clock numbers.

Glue cardboard to knitted clock.

Make a hole in clock center and push shaft of clock battery back through the hole.

Lay the clock gently on top of shaft and ease shaft through center.

Attach hands according to package directions.

knitted clock

This stockinette hood provides a cozy alternative to a traditional winter hat. Seed stitch edging adds a decorative element, and keeps the borders from rolling.

## materials

5 balls in #200 Prairie of Fettuccini by Lion Brand, 1¾oz/50g balls, each approx 33yd/30m (wool/acrylic/nylon)

One pair size 15 (10mm) needles OR SIZE TO OBTAIN GAUGE

2yd/2m of ³⁄₁₆"/5mm nylon cord

Single-hole plastic cord stopper

Large safety pin

## finished measurements

Approx 10"/25.5cm wide, 10"/25.5cm long and 6"/15cm deep (excluding collar)

## the gauge

8 sts and 13 rows to 4"/10cm over St st using size 15 (10mm) needles. BE SURE TO GET THE GAUGE.

**Note:** See Chapter 10 for instructions on how to pick up stitches.

## seed stitch

**Row 1** *K1, p1; rep from * to end. **Row 2** K the p sts and P the k sts. Rep row 2 for seed st.

## make the hood

■ **Make two side panels.** Cast on 18 sts. Work in St st until piece measures 10"/25.5cm from beg, end with a WS row. Bind off.

■ **Make center panel.** Cast on 10 sts. Work in seed stitch until piece measures 18"/45.5cm from beg, end with a WS row. Bind off.

## finish the hood

■ For right side panel, pin left side edge and bound-off edge of one side panel to center panel, matching cast-on edges of both pieces. Sew in place. For left side panel, pin right side edge and bound-off edge of remaining side panel to center panel, matching cast-on edges of both pieces. Sew in place.

■ **Make the drawstring casing**. With RS facing, pick up and k 18 sts evenly spaced across right side edge of right side panel, 7 sts across bound-off edge of center panel and 18 sts across left side edge of left side panel—43 sts. Work in garter st for 8 rows. Bind off all sts knitwise. Fold casing in half to WS and sew in place.

■ **Make the collar**. With RS facing, pick up and k 25 sts evenly spaced across cast-on edges, beg after drawstring casing on one side and ending before drawstring casing on opposite side. **Row 1** K2tog, k to last 2 sts, ssk. **Row 2** Knit. Rep these 2 rows twice more, then row 1 once. Bind off rem 17 sts knitwise. Attach safety pin to one end of nylon cord. Thread cord through drawstring casing; remove safety pin. Thread both cord ends through cord stopper. Cut cord ends to desired length. Knot cord ends.

Unless you want to spend the rest of your knitting career stitching squares and rectangles, you'll need to learn how to **increase** and **decrease**. This is a simple matter of **dropping** and **adding** stitches from and to the needle, so that you can add and subtract inches to the knitted piece. There are a number of ways to do this (aren't there always?); we're going to show you a few of the most common. Let's start with two decreases: **Knit two together** and **purl two together** (a.k.a. k2tog and p2tog). They sound a lot more complicated than they are. Really.

# Increases   and   Decreases

**1.** Insert the right needle from front to back (knitwise) into the next two stitches on the left needle. Wrap the yarn around the right needle (as when knitting) and pull it through. You have decreased one stitch.

**2.** Insert the right needle into the front loops (purlwise) of the next two stitches on the left needle. Wrap the yarn around the right needle (as when purling) and pull it through. You have decreased one stitch.

k2tog

p2tog

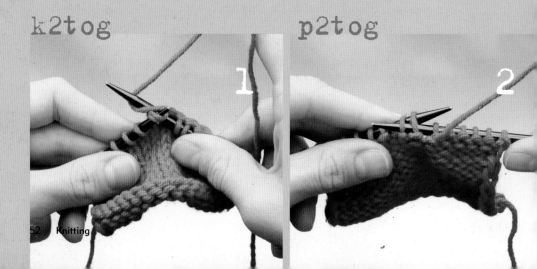

bar increase

Now let's try the **increase**. One of our favorites is the bar increase made by working into the front and back loops of the same stitch. It leaves a small, slightly visible bar that you can hide in a seam or embrace as a design element. Here's how:

**3.** Insert the right needle knitwise into the stitch to be increased. Wrap the yarn around the right needle and pull it through as if knitting, but leave the stitch on the left needle.

**4.** Insert the right needle into the back of the same stitch. Wrap the yarn around the needle and pull it through. Slip the stitch off the left needle. You now have two stitches on the right needle.

## tip

Working increases and decreases on the right side of the work allows you to see the finished look and makes it easier to keep track of how many stitches you've added or subtracted.

Now quit being being so square. Let's put those increases and decreases to work in a few shapely projects.

These eye-catching plant cozies will allow you to experiment with color while "increasing" your knitting skills. They're knit flat in stockinette stitch and seamed to form tubes.

# plant cozies

## materials

1 ball each in #116 Delft Blue, #176 Spring Green, #123 Seaspray, #148 Turquoise and #146 Lilac of Wool-Ease® by Lion Brand, 3oz/85g balls, each approx 197yds/180m (80%acrylic/20% wool)

One pair size 8 (5mm) needles OR SIZE TO OBTAIN GAUGE

## finished measurements

**Small** cozy is 12"/30.5cm around by 2¼"/6cm high. **Large** cozy is 17"/43 cm around by 5½"/14cm high.

## the gauge

16 sts and 25 rows to 4"/10cm over St st using size 8 (5mm) needles.

BE SURE TO GET THE GAUGE.

## make the small cozy

### 2-color version

■ With Spring Green, cast on 38 sts. Working in stripe pat of [2 rows Spring Green, 2 rows Turquoise 3 times, 2 rows Spring Green, work as foll:

■ Work in St st for 2 rows. **Next (inc) row (RS)** K1, inc 1 st in next st, k to last 2 sts, inc 1 st in next st, k1. Purl 1 row. Rep last 2 rows 4 times more—48 sts. Work 2 rows even. Bind off purlwise on RS.

### Rainbow-colored version

■ With Delft Blue, cast on 38 sts. Working shaping as for the 2-color style, work stripes as foll: Work 3 rows Delft Blue, 2 rows Lilac, 2 rows Turquoise, 2 rows Spring Green, 2 rows Seaspray, 2 rows Delft Blue, 1 row Lilac. Bind off purlwise on RS with Lilac.

## make the large cozy

■ With Delft Blue, cast on 60 sts. Work in st st for 2 rows.

■ **Next (inc) row (RS)** K1, inc 1 st in next st, k to last 2 sts, inc 1 st in next st, k1. Purl 1 row. Rep the last 2 rows 13 times more—88 sts. Work in St st for 2 rows. Bind off purlwise on RS.

## finish the cozies

■ Join the short edges of cozy tog to form the tube that fits around the flowerpot.

This ribbon vest is a wardrobe essential.
Ribbing, shaping, color, texture and
pattern—it's got it all!

## materials

4 (5, 6) balls in #208 Copper Penny of Incredible by Lion Brand, 1¾oz/50g
balls, each approx 110yd/100m (nylon)
One size 13 (9mm) circular needles OR SIZE TO OBTAIN GAUGE
Stitch markers
Sized for Small (Medium, Large). Shown in size Small.

## finished measurements

**Bust** 32 (34, 36)"/81 (86, 91.5)cm
**Length** 15 (15¾, 16¼)"/38 (40, 41)cm

## the gauge

25 sts to 8"/20.5cm and 18 rows to 4"/10cm over pat st using size 13 (9mm)
needles. BE SURE TO GET THE GAUGE.

## pattern stitch

**Row 1 (RS)** Knit. **Rows 2, 4, 6 and 8** Purl. **Row 3** *K1, p1; rep from * to
end. **Row 5** Knit. **Row 7** *P1, k1; rep from * to end. Rep rows 1–8 for pat st.

## make the body

Cast on 100 (106, 112) sts. **Row 1 (RS)** K23 (24, 26), pm, k 54 (58, 60), pm, k
23 (24, 26). Cont in pat st until piece measures 5¼ (5½, 5¾)"/13.5 (14, 14.5)cm
from beg.

## shape the neck

Dec 1 st each end of next row then every other row 5 times more, every 4th row
5 times, AT SAME TIME, when piece measures 6¼ (6½, 6¾)"/16 (16.5, 17)cm from
beg, work as foll:

## shape the armhole

**Next row (RS)** Work to 1 st before the first marker, bind off 2 sts for
armhole, work to 1 st before the 2nd marker, bind off 2 sts, work to end. Work
segments separately as foll:

## make the right front

■ Cont the front neck shaping, dec 1 st at armhole edge every other row 4 (5, 7) times, every 4th row 5 times—2 sts rem after all shaping. Work even, if necessary, until armhole measures 6¾ (7¼, 7½)"/17 (18.5, 19)cm. Bind off.

## make the left front

■ Rejoin yarn and work as for right front, reversing shaping.

## make the back

■ Rejoin yarn and cont to shape armholes, dec 1 st at each end every other row 4 (6, 7) times, every 4th row 5 times, AT SAME TIME, when armhole measures 5½ (6, 6¼)"/14 (15, 16)cm, bind off center 20 sts and working both sides at once, bind off 3 sts from each neck edge once, 2 sts twice.

## make armhole edge

■ Sew side seams. Pick up and k 42 (45, 48) sts evenly around armholes. (See chapter 10, p.106 for how to pick up stitches). Bind off knitwise.

## finish the vest

■ Place yarn markers at center front at 4"/10cm from lower edge, 7"/18cm from the first marker and mark the opposite center front in same way. Beg at right side seam, pick up and k 77 (81, 85) sts to right front corner, 1 st at corner, pm, 12 sts from corner to first marker, 18 sts to next marker, 8 (10, 12) sts to shoulder, cast on 4 sts at shoulder, 33 sts across back neck, cast on 4 sts at shoulder, 8 (10, 12) sts to marker, 18 sts to next marker, 12 sts to corner, 1 st at corner, pm, 18 (20, 22) sts to beg of rnd—214 (224, 234) sts.

■ Join and *work in k1, p1 rib to the marked corner st, inc 1 st each side of the corner st; rep from * then rib to end. Rep this inc every other row until rib measures 1¾"/4.5cm. Bind off.

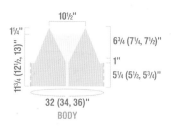

10½"

1¼"

11¾ (12½, 13)"

6¾ (7¼, 7½)"

1"

5¼ (5½, 5¾)"

32 (34, 36)"
BODY

## materials

9 (11, 13, 15) balls in #099 Fisherman of Jiffy® by Lion Brand, 3oz/85g balls, each approx 135yd/123m (acrylic)

One pair size 10 (6 mm) needles OR SIZE TO OBTAIN GAUGE

Sized for Small (Medium, Large, X- Large). Shown in size Medium.

## finished measurements

**Bust** 34 (38, 42, 46)"/86.5 (96.5, 106.5, 117)cm

**Length** 23½ (24, 24½, 25)"/59.5 (61, 62, 63.5)cm

**Upper arm** 12 (13, 14, 15)"/30.5 (33, 35.5, 38)cm

## the gauge

14½ sts and 28 rows to 4"/10cm over garter st using size 10 (6mm) needles. BE SURE TO GET THE GAUGE.

## make the back

■ Cast on 62 (69, 76, 83) sts. Work in garter stitch for 16"/40.5cm.

## shape the armhole

■ Bind off 3 (4, 4, 5) sts at beg of next 2 rows, 2 sts at beg of next 0 (0, 2, 2) rows, then dec 1 st each side every other row 4 (5, 5, 5) times— 48 (51, 54, 59) sts. Work even until armhole measures 6 (6½, 7, 7½)"/15 (16.5, 17.5, 19)cm.

## shape the neck

■ **Next row (RS)** K 11 (12, 13, 15) sts, join 2nd ball of yarn and bind off center 26 (27, 28, 29) sts, work to end. Working both sides at once, dec 1 st at each neck edge every other row 4 times. Work even until armhole measures 7½ (8, 8½, 9)"/19 (20.5, 21.5, 23)cm. Bind off rem 7 (8, 9, 11) sts each side for shoulders.

## make the sleeves

■ Cast on 44 (48, 51, 55) sts. Work in garter st for 18 (18½, 18½, 19)"/45.5 (47, 47, 48.4)cm.

## make the front

■ Work same as the back.

## make the sleeves

■ Cast on 44 (48, 51, 55) sts. Work in garter st for 18 (18½, 18½, 19)"/45.5 (47, 47, 48.4)cm.

## shape the cap

■ Bind off 3 (4, 4, 5) sts at beg of next 2 rows. Dec 1 st each side every other row 10 (10, 11, 11) times, every 4th row 2 (3, 3, 4) times. Bind off 2 sts at beg of next 2 rows. Bind off rem 10 (10, 11, 11) sts.

## make the collar

■ Cast on 80 sts. Work in k1, p1 ribbing for 21"/53.5cm. Bind off loosely in ribbing.

## finish the sweater

■ Sew shoulder seams. Set in sleeves. Sew side and sleeve seams.

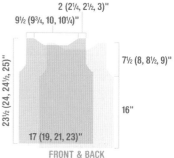

2 (2¼, 2½, 3)"
9½ (9¾, 10, 10¼)"
7½ (8, 8½, 9)"
23½ (24, 24½, 25)"
16"
17 (19, 21, 23)"
FRONT & BACK

4½ (5, 5½, 6)"
18 (18½, 18½, 19)"
12 (13, 14, 15)"
SLEEVES

A voluminous cowl collar highlights this comfy garter-stitch pullover. You'll be anxious to get this design off the needles so you can wear it all season long.

Now that you are knitting and purling your way through all sorts of projects and patterns, let's up the ante by introducing techiques a little (but only a little!) more complicated: yarn overs and cables.

# Yarn Overs

Yarn overs (YO in pattern lingo) are really just increases that leave a little hole in your knitting. "Umm…aren't holes a bad thing?" you ask. When they are the result of an unintentionally dropped stitch, yes. But when you make the holes intentionally, what you have, ladies (and any gentlemen who may be reading), is a lovely lace or eyelet pattern. Here's how they work:

Between two knit stitches. Yarn over by bringing the yarn from the back of the work to the front between the two needles. Knit the next stitch, bringing the yarn to the back over the right needle.

# Cables

Cables are those beautiful winding, rope-like designs we all associate with fisherman's sweaters and preppy crew necks. They're gorgeous, magical and incredibly intimidating to the new knitter. But we're going to let you in on a secret. Cables really aren't that complicated. Honest. Would we lie? To make cables, you will need a small, double-pointed

needle called a cable needle. Cable needles work as placeholders for stitches you need to come back to. By knitting "out of order," we can create an intriguing twisted effect. Most cables are worked as knit stitches over a purl background, and many come with a chart. Take your first baby step by knitting this cable:

## Giant cables

**Right cable**

(panel of 16 sts)

**12-st right cable** Sl 6 sts to cn and hold to back of work, k6, k6 from cn.

**Rows 1 and 3 (RS)** P2, k12, p2.

**Row 2 and all WS rows** K the knit sts and p the purl sts.

**Row 5** P2, 12-st right cable, p2.

**Row 7** Rep row 1.

**Row 8** Rep row 2.

Rep rows 1–8.

**Left cable**

(panel of 16 sts)

**12-st left cable** Sl 6 sts to cn and hold to front of work, k6, k6 from cn.

**Rows 1 and 3 (RS)** P2, k12, p2.

**Row 2 and all WS rows** K the knit sts and p the purl sts.

**Row 5** P2, 12-st left cable, p2.

**Row 7** Rep row 1.

**Row 8** Rep row 2.

Rep rows 1–8.

See, that wasn't so bad, was it? Now let's put those newfound skills to work….

## tip

First-timers often forget and drop the extra stitch created by the yarn over on the next row. Make sure you knit or purl the stitch as the pattern requires.

These picot-edge gauntlets are a fast, fun knit featuring eyelet trim (love those yo's!). Make a bunch of these in different colors—they make great gifts (if you can bear to part with them).

## materials

1 ball in #153 Ebony of Microspun by Lion Brand, 2½oz/70g ball, each approx 168yd/154m (micro-fiber acrylic)
One pair size 6 (4mm) needles OR SIZE TO OBTAIN GAUGE
Stitch markers

## the measurements

**Width** around hand 7¼"/18.5cm
**Length** 7½"/19cm

## the gauge

20 sts and 28 rows to 4"/10cm over St st using size 6 (4mm)
needles. BE SURE TO GET THE GAUGE.

## make the gauntlets (make 2)

■ Beg at cuff edge, cast on 42 sts.

■ **Rows 1–4** Work even in St st. **Row 5** (turning row) K1, *yo, k2tog; rep from * to last st, k1. **Rows 6–9** Work even in St st. **Row 10 (WS)** K2, *p3, k2; rep from * to end. **Row 11** P2, *k1, yo, ssk, p2; rep from * to end. **Row 12** Rep row 10. **Row 13** P2, *k2tog, yo, k1, p2; rep from * to end. **Row 14** Rep row 10. Rep rows 11–14 for 5 times more. Work 5 rows in St st.

## make the thumb gusset

■ **Next row (WS)** P20, pm, p2, pm, p20. **Next row (RS)** K20, sl marker, m1, k to marker, m1, sl marker, k20. **Next row (WS)** P to marker, sl marker, k to marker, sl marker, p to end. Rep last 2 rows 5 times more—54 sts. **Next row (RS)** K20, bind off 14 sts, k to end—40sts. Work 3 rows in St st. Work 6 rows in garter st. Bind off all sts.

## finish the gauntlet

■ Turn the lower edge at the turning row and seam to WS for picot edging.
■ Sew side seam.

These laced-up leggings are a stylish blend of old and new. Traditional wool and timeless eyelet patterning are paired with fashion-forward leather laces and novelty yarn cuffs. This project is sure to get—and keep—your attention.

## materials

3 skeins in #099 Fisherman of Wool-Ease® by Lion Brand, 3oz/85g skeins, each approx 197yd/180m (wool/acrylic)

6 skeins in #098 Ivory of Fun Fur by Lion Brand, 1¾ oz/50g skeins, each approx 60yd/54m (polyester)

One pair each sizes 10½ and size 13 (6.5 and 9 mm) needles OR SIZE TO OBTAIN GAUGE

Two leather boot straps

## the measurements

**Circumference at widest point** 13"/33cm
**Length with cuff turned down** 33"/83.5cm

## the gauge

16 sts and 24 rows to 4"/10cm over pattern stitch using size 10½ (6.5 mm) needles and Wool-Ease. BE SURE TO GET THE GAUGE.

## make the leggings

■ With Wool-Ease, Fisherman and size 10½ (6.5 mm) needles, cast on 52 sts. **Row 1 (WS)** Sl 1, p2, *k2, p2; rep from *, end k1. **Row 2** Sl 1, k1, yo, k1, *p2, k2; rep from * to last 5 sts, p2, k1, yo, k2. **Row 3** Sl 1, p3, *k2, p2; rep from * to last 6 sts., k2, p3, k1. **Row 4** Sl 1, k1, k2tog, *p2, k2; rep from * to last 6 sts, p2, k1, k2tog, k1. **Row 5** Sl 1, *p2, k2; rep from * to last 3 sts, p2, k1. **Row 6** Sl 1, *k2, p2; rep from *, to last 3 sts, k3. **Row 7** Rep row 1. **Row 8** Sl 1, *k1, yo, k1, p2; rep from *, to last 3 sts, k1, yo, k2. **Row 9** Sl 1, *p3, k2; rep from *, to last 4 sts, p3, k1. **Row 10** Sl 1, *k1, k2tog, p2; rep from *, to last 4 sts, k1, k2tog, k1. **Row 11** Sl 1, *p2, k1, yo, k1; rep from * to last 3 sts, p2, k1. **Row 12** Sl 1, *k2, p3; rep from * to last 3 sts, k3. **Row 13** Sl 1, *p2, k1, k2tog; rep from * to last 3 sts, p2, k1. Rep rows 8–13 nine times (or to desired length right about at the knee). Bind off.

## make the cuff

■ With 2 strands of Fun Fur and size 13 (9 mm) needles, pick up sts along lower edge (approx at the knee) as follows: *pick up 1 st in first st, 1 st in 2nd st and 2 sts in 3rd st; rep from * across. Cont to work in garter stitch, for the desired length (sample shown is a bit longer than the knitted rib part). Bind off all sts.

## finish the leggings

■ With leather boot straps, lace up the sides of each legging (see photo).

These snug leg warmers feature a classic cable pattern bordered by ribbing at ankle and thigh. Knit in the round, they work up quickly.

## materials

3 skeins in #99 Fisherman of Wool-Ease® Chunky by Lion Brand, 5oz/140g skeins, each approx 153yds/140m (acrylic/wool)

One size 9 (5.5mm) circular needle, 12"/30.5cm length OR SIZE TO OBTAIN GAUGE

Cable needle (cn) and stitch marker

## the measurements

**Thigh circumference** (fully stretched) 18"/45.5cm

**Length** 27"/68.5cm

## the gauge

■ 16 sts and 18 rows to 4"/10cm over cable pat using size 9 (5.5mm) needles. BE SURE TO GET THE GAUGE.

**Stitch glossary**

**6-st RC** Slip 3 sts to cn and hold to back, k3, k3 from cn.

**6-st LC** Slip 3 sts to cn and hold to front, k3, k3 from cn.

**Cable pattern**

(mult of 14 sts)

**Rnds 1, 2, 4, 5, 6, 7** *K12, p2; rep from * to end of rnd. **Rnd 3** *6-st RC, 6-st LC, p2; rep from * to end of rnd. **Rnd 8** *K12, p2; rep from * to end of rnd. Rep rnds 1–8 for Cable Pattern.

## make the leg warmers (make 2)

■ Cast on 44 sts, place marker and join for knitting in the round, taking care not to twist sts. Work in k2, p2 rib for 2"/5cm. **Next rnd** K2tog, k20, k2tog, knit to end of rnd—42 sts. **Next rnd** Work rnd 1 of 14-st Cable Pattern 3 times. Cont in Cable Pattern for 18"/45.5cm. **Next rnd (inc)** *K12 in pat, p1, m1, p1; rep from * to end of rnd—45 sts. Work in pats and cont to inc 1 st in each purl section every other rnd 3 times more—54sts. Work even in pats until piece measures 23"/58.5cm. **Next rnd (dec)** K2tog, k25, k2tog, knit to end—52 sts. Work in k2, p2 rib for 4½"/12cm. Bind off in rib.

You haven't exactly been knitting in black and white, but up to this point, the scene has been a bit monotone. So let's work on livening things up with an introduction to colorwork.

# Show Your Stripes

**Stripes** are the easiest way to introduce a little color into your knitting. Basically, you just knit a few rows to the width you want, then change to a new color when you're ready for a different stripe. (For info on how to do this, see "Joining Yarn" on page 22). There's no complicated color changing mid-row, and you can simply carry the colors along the side when you switch to a new stripe. You'll see how simple this is below:

## Carrying colors along the side

**1.** When changing colors with narrow, even-numbered stripes, drop the old color. Bring the new color under the old color, being sure not to pull the yarn too tightly, and knit the next stripe.

**2.** When working thicker stripes (generally more than four rows), carry the old yarn up the side until it is needed again by twisting the working yarn around the old yarn every couple of rows, as shown.

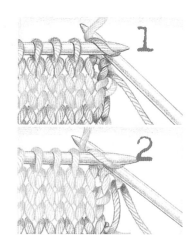

# Fair Play

**Fair Isle**, also known as stranded knitting, takes its name from the remote British Isle where the style developed. Many moons ago, the local women started stitching great geometrically patterned designs that were doubly warm, thanks to the strands of wool carried across the back of the sweater as the patterns were knit. They're still doing it today, running a literal cottage industry with yarn and needles.

These days the term refers to any kind of colorwork characterized by small repeated patterns, and it's a lot easier to accomplish than it looks. Multiple colors are used in the design, but only two colors are used in any one row. As you stitch across the row, you use only the color called for in the pattern and carry the other color loosely across the back. Watch and learn as we explain in more detail:

## Stranding: one-handed

**1.** On the knit side, drop the working yarn. Bring the new color (now the working yarn) over the top of the dropped yarn and work to the next color change.

**2.** Drop the working yarn. Bring the new color under the dropped yarn and work to the next color change. Repeat steps 1 and 2.

**3.** On the purl side, drop the working yarn. Bring the new color (now the working yarn) over the top of the dropped yarn and work to the next color change.

**4.** Drop the working yarn. Bring the new color under the dropped yarn and work to the next color change. Repeat steps 3 and 4.

If you are going to be working more than four stitches between color changes, it's advisable to **weave** or **twist** the color not being used into or under the stitches. If you don't do this, you risk catching the long, loose floats on fingers, jewelry, belly rings or belt buckles. Here's how:

## Weaving above a knit stitch

**1.** Hold the working yarn in your right hand and the yarn to be woven in your left. To weave the yarn above a knit stitch, bring it over the right needle. Knit the stitch with the working yarn, bringing it under the woven yarn.

**2.** The woven yarn will go under the next knit stitch. With the working yarn, knit the stitch, bringing the yarn over the woven yarn. Repeat steps 1 and 2 to the next color change.

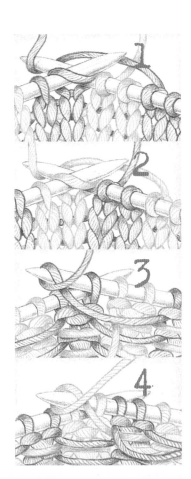

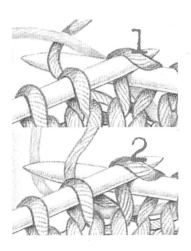

## Weaving above a purl stitch

**1.** To weave the yarn above a purl stitch, bring it over the right needle. Purl the stitch with the working yarn, bringing it under the woven yarn.

**2.** To weave the yarn below a purl stitch, purl the stitch with the working yarn, bringing it over the woven yarn. Repeat steps 1 and 2 to the next color change.

## Twisting

**1.** On the knit side, twist the working yarn and the carried yarn around each other once. Then continue knitting with the same color as before.

**2.** On the purl side, twist the yarns around each other as shown, then continue purling with the same color as before.

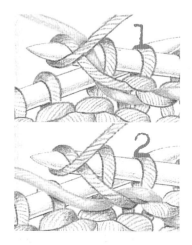 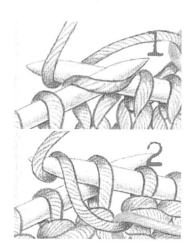

# tip

It can be awkward to work with lots of big balls of color (quit snickering, we're talking yarn here) so keep things from tangling by using bobbins for intarsia work. Knit along with the first color; then when you get to the change, unroll a good quantity of yarn and wind it around a plastic bobbin or create a little butterfly (see photo on page 76). Do this at each color change and you'll find things go much more smoothly. If the bobbins start tangling, try breaking off a length of each color (one the length of your arm should do it) and let it hang down behind your work. That way when you need a certain color you can just pull it free from the rest.

# Picture This

Now on to **intarsia**, which involves large blocks of single colors worked with separate balls of yarn. These can create a picture (heart, flower, pirate skull, or what ever else strikes your fancy), or an abstract or geometric design.

Since the designs are worked over large areas, it's not practical to carry yarn across the back of the work (you'd end up with a tangled mess, not to mention waste a lot of yarn), so you twist the different colors around each other at each color change to prevent holes.

Allow us to demonstrate:

## Changing colors in a vertical line

1. On the knit side, drop the old color. Pick up the new color from under the old color and knit to the next color change.

2. On the purl side, drop the old color. Pick up the new color from under the old color and purl to the next color change. Repeat steps 1 and 2.

## Changing colors in a diagonal line when working a right diagonal

1. On the knit side, bring the new color over the top of the old color and knit to the next color change.

2. On the purl side, pick up the new color from under the old color and purl to the next color change.

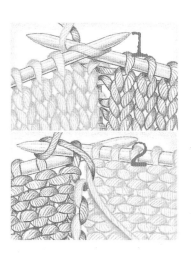

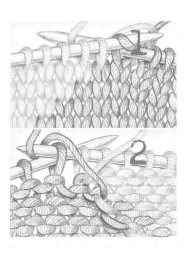

## Changing colors in a diagonal line when working a left diagonal

1. On the purl side, bring the new color over the top of the old color and purl to the next color change.

2. On the knit side, pick up the new color from under the old color and knit to the next color change.

## Joining a new color: Version A

1. Wrap first the old and then the new yarn knitwise and work the first stitch with both yarns.

2. Drop the old yarn. Work the next two stitches with both ends of the new yarn.

3. Drop the short end of the new color and continue working with the single strand. On the following rows, work the three double stitches as single stitches.

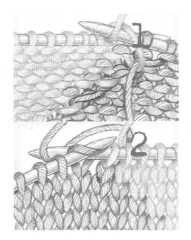

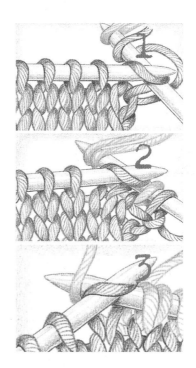

## tip

When changing colors, always twist the yarns on the wrong side to prevent holes in the work.

## Joining a new color: Version B

1. Cut the old yarn, leaving about 4 inches (10cm). Purl the first two stitches with the new yarn. *Insert the needle purlwise into the stitch, lay the short ends of both the old and new colors over the top of the needle, and purl the next stitch under the short ends.

2. Leave the short ends hanging and purl the next stitch over them.

3. Repeat from the * until you have woven the short ends into the wrong side of the piece.

## Joining a new color: Version C

1. Work to three stitches before where you want to join the new yarn. Work these stitches with the yarn folded double, making sure you have just enough to work three stitches.

2. Loop the new yarn into the loop of the old yarn, leaving the new yarn doubled for about 8 inches (20cm). Knit the next three stitches with the doubled yarn. Let the short end of the new yarn hang and continue knitting with one strand.

3. On the next row, carry the first yarn across the back of the work from where it was dropped on the previous row and twist it together with the second yarn. Work the doubled stitches as single stitches.

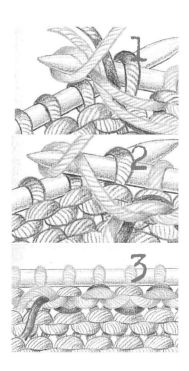

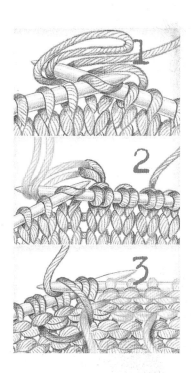

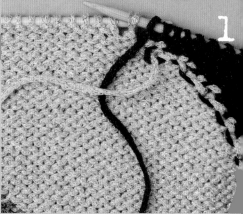

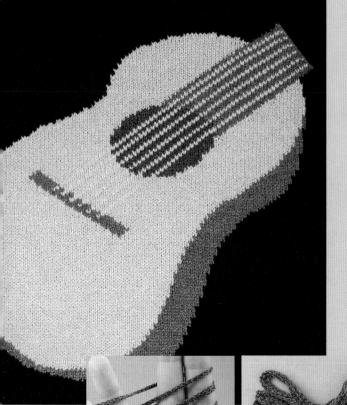

Warhol used silkscreen; **knitters** use **yarn**. Paint a picture with intarsia knitting. (Guitar Sweater pattern featured on p.84.)

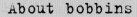

## About bobbins

Make your own "butterfly" bobbins: Hold the end of the yarn with your thumb. Wrap the yarn in a figure eight around your fingers as shown, then wrap the tail around the center and tie. Pull the yarn from the original tail.

Purchased bobbins, like the transparent ones shown above, prevent the different strands from getting tangled.

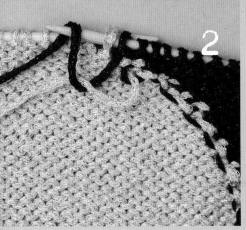

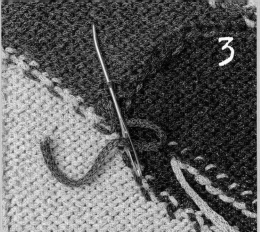

Get

## Get Started

1. The next stitch is worked with black. Lay the gold yarn over top of the black.

2. Bring the black over top of the gold and purl the next stitch. Keep the floats neat, tugging the yarn a little (but not too much, or the fabric will pucker). A good tip: "Old color over new color."

3. After all the pieces have been knit, and before blocking and seaming, weave the extra ends into the wrong side. Thread the end into a tapestry needle, insert the needle into a loop near the end, then insert it into the next stitch in the

opposite direction. Weave the strand in this way over several stitches, then cut it.

4. For small areas of color, embroider the stitches with duplicate stitch instead of knitting them in. Insert the tapestry needle from the back to the front in the center "V" of a stitch, then under the two loops of the same stitch one row above; pull through.

5. Insert the needle back into the center where the needle first came out to complete the stitch.

Now that you've got a general grip on the basics of colorwork, let's work it into a few projects.

These leg warmers are a great first project for trying out colorwork. The unmatched stripes keep the knitting interesting, and should your row count vary a bit from the pattern—well, who's to know?

## materials

1 ball each in #152 Charcoal and #112 Red of Wool-Ease® Chunky by Lion Brand, 5oz/140g balls, each approx 153yd/140m (acrylic/wool)

One pair size 10½ (6.5mm) needles OR SIZE TO OBTAIN GAUGE

## finished measurements

Approx 9"/23cm wide at top edge and 14½"/37cm long

## the gauge

14 sts and 16 rows to 4"/10cm over St st using size 10½ (6.5mm) needles. BE SURE TO GET THE GAUGE.

## make the leg warmer 1

■ With Charcoal, cast on 31 sts. Work in k1, p1 rib for 7 rows.

Purl 1 row. **Inc row (RS)** K2, inc 1 st in next st, k to last 3 sts, inc 1 st in next st, k2—33 sts. Purl 1 row. With Red, k1 row, p1 row. With Charcoal, rep inc row—35 sts. Then work 5 more rows in St st with Charcoal. With Red, work 2 rows in St st. With Charcoal, work 6 rows in St st. Rep the last 8 rows twice more. **Dec row (RS)** With Red, k2, ssk, k to last 4 sts, k2tog, k2—33 sts. Purl 1 row. Cont to work the 8-row stripe pat, rep dec row every 6th row once more—31 sts. Work even until there are a total of 6 reps of 8-row stripe pat. With Charcoal, purl 1 row on RS. Bind off knitwise, leaving a long end.

## finish the leg warmer

■ Sew back seam of leg warmer.

## make the leg warmer 2

■ **Note** The stripe pat is 4 rows Red, 4 rows Charcoal. Rep these 8 rows for stripe pat.

■ With Charcoal, cast on 31 sts. Work in k1, p1 rib for 7 rows.

Purl 1 row. **Inc row (RS)** With Red, k2, inc 1 st in next st, k to last 3 sts, inc 1 st in next st, k2—33 sts. Purl 1 row, k1 row, p1 row. With Charcoal, rep inc row—35 sts. Cont to work in 8-row stripe pat for 29 rows more. **Dec row (RS)** With Red, k2, ssk, k to last 4 sts, k2tog, k2—33 sts. Cont to work the 8-row stripe pat, rep dec row every 6th row once more—31 sts. Work even until there is a total of 6 reps of 8-row stripe pat. With Red, work 4 rows in St st. With Charcoal, purl 1 row on RS. Bind off knitwise, leaving a long end.

## finish the leg warmer

■ Sew back seam of leg warmer.

striped leg warmers

This project gives new meaning to the idea of "knitting for relaxation." Decorative clouds are duplicate stitched prior to stuffing and seaming the knitted pieces. Buttons complete the finished look.

## materials

1 ball each in #105 Light Blue (MC) and #98 Cream (CC) of Lion Cashmere Blend by Lion Brand, 1½ oz/40g skeins, each approx 84yd/77m (merino wool/nylon/cashmere)

One pair size 7 (4.5mm) knitting needles OR SIZE TO OBTAIN GAUGE

Crochet hook size H/8 (5mm)

Stitch holder

Yarn needle

½yd fleece fabric

Sewing thread

Buckwheat hulls or fiberfill stuffing

3½" (13mm) pearl buttons

## finished measurements

**Width** 13"/33cm

**Length** 12"/30.5cm

## the gauge

17 sts and 25 rows to 4"/10 cm over St st using size 8 (5 mm)

needles. BE SURE TO GET THE GAUGE.

**Note** Clouds are embroidered in duplicate st after front piece has been knitted. When referring to "right" front or "left" front, we're talking about the neck pillow as it is worn.

## make the right front

■ With MC, cast on 7 sts. **Rows 1, 3, 5 (RS)** Inc, k to last st, inc. **Rows 2 and 4** Inc, p to last st, inc. **Row 6** Purl. Rep rows 5–6 three times more—23 sts. Work 12 rows even in St st. **Row 25 (RS)** Inc, k across. Work 3 rows even in St st. **Row 29 (RS)** Rep row 25. **Row 30** Purl. **Row 31** Rep row 25. **Row 32** Purl across to last st, inc—27 sts. Place all sts on holder.

## make the left front and complete front

7

1

10 sts

color key

■ light blue

▨ cream

## make the left front and complete front

■ Work as for rows 1–32 of right front, reversing all shaping, do not put sts on holder.

**Row 33 (RS)** Knit to end, cast on 4 sts, k across 27 sts on holder—58 sts. Work 19 rows even in St st.

**Row 53 (RS)** Ssk, k to last 2 sts, k2tog—56 sts. Work 3 rows even in St st.

**Row 57 (RS)** Rep row 53—54 sts. Work 1 row even in St st. Rep last 2 rows 4 times more—46 sts. **Row 67** Rep row 53—44 sts.

**Row 68** P2tog, p across, ssp—42 sts. Rep last 2 rows once more—38 sts. Bind off 4 sts at beg of next 2 rows, 6 sts at beg of next 2 rows. Bind off rem 18 sts.

## make the bottom back

**Note** Back is made in 2 pieces.

■ With CC, work as for front through row 52. **Rows 53–56** Work in k1, p1 rib. Bind off.

## make the top back

■ With CC, cast on 58 sts. **Rows 1–4** Work in k1, p1 rib. **Row 5** (buttonhole row) [K13, k2tog, yo] 3 times, k13. **Row 6** Purl. Complete to match front, starting with row 53.

## finish the pillow cover

■ Steam all pieces. Using CC and yarn needle, follow chart to embroider clouds in duplicate stitch, spacing them randomly over front (our sample has 7 clouds, 3 of which are reversed image of chart). Trace around front to make a liner pattern. Cut out 2 identical liner pieces from fleece fabric and sew tog leaving a gap for stuffing. Clip seams and turn right side out, stuffing with buckwheat hulls or fiberfill. Sew gap. Pin knitted back pieces to front, overlapping ribbed edge of top back over ribbed edge of lower back. With MC, crochet hook and front facing, work a rnd of sc around entire edge, followed by 2 rnds of sl st. Fasten off. Sew buttons on ribbed edge of bottom back. Place stuffed pillow inside cover.

Sparkle like a pop star in this shimmery raglan-sleeve pullover knit in "Glitterspun." The strings of the intarsia guitar are worked later in duplicate stitch (see pages 76 and 77 for our technique workshop).

## materials

7 skeins in #153 Onyx, 2 skeins in #170 Gold, 1 skein each in #135 Bronze, #144 Amethyst, #150 Silver of Glitterspun by Lion Brand, 1¾oz/50g skeins, each approx 115yd/105m (acrylic/polyester/cupro)

One pair size 7 (4.5mm) knitting needles OR SIZE TO OBTAIN GAUGE

Crochet hook size G/6 (4mm), tapestry needle and stitch holder

## finished measurements

**Bust** 34 (37, 40)"/86.5 (94, 101.5)cm
**Length** 24¼ (24¾, 25½)"/61.5 (63, 64.5)cm
**Upperarm** 13½ (14½, 15½)"/34.5 (37, 39.5)cm

## the gauge

20 sts and 28 rows to 4"/10cm over St st using size 7 (4.5mm) needles.
BE SURE TO GET THE GAUGE.

## note

■ When changing colors, twist yarns on WS to prevent holes in work. Make separate bobbins for each block of color. If desired, the strings of the guitar can worked in Duplicate stitch after pieces are knit, as were done in this sample. See pages 76 and 77 for Color Workshop.

## make the front

■ With Onyx and size 7 (4.5mm) needles, cast on 86 (92, 100) sts. Work in k1, p1 rib for 5 rows. Beg with a purl row and work in St st for 3 rows.

## work the chart

■ **Next row (RS)** Beg and end as indicated, work in chart pat through row 100. Piece measures approx 15½"/39.5cm from beg.

## shape the raglan armholes and neck

■ Work armhole shaping as shown on chart as follows: Bind off 2 sts at beg of next 2 rows—82 (88, 96) sts. **Row 1 (RS)** K1, ssk, k to last 3 sts, k2tog, k1. **Row 2** P1, p2 tog, p to last 3 sts, p2tog tbl, p1. **Row 3 (RS)** K1, ssk, k to last 3 sts, k2tog, k1. **Row 4 (WS)** Purl all sts—76 (82, 90) sts. **Next row (RS)** K1, ssk, k to last 3 sts, k2tog, k1. **Next row** Purl. Repeat last two rows 22 (24, 27) times more, AT THE SAME TIME, on chart row 137 (141, 147), work neck shaping as foll: **Next row (RS)** Bind off center 6 (8, 10) sts for neck and working both sides at once, bind off from each neck edge 3 sts once, 2 sts once, dec 1 st every other row once, every 3 sts each side.

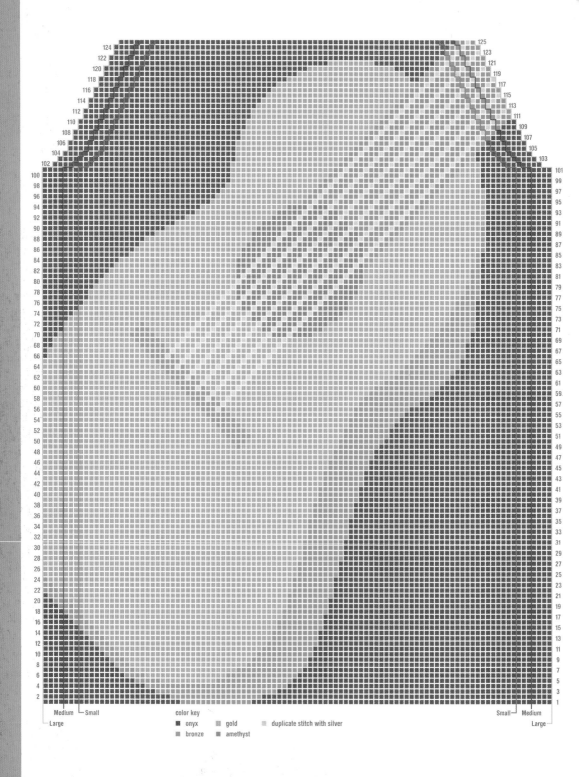

## make the back

▓ With Onyx and size 7 (4.5mm) needles, cast on 92 sts. Work as for front with Onyx only (omitting chart pat) until same length as back to armhole.

## shape the raglan armholes

▓ Work as for front, omitting neck shaping. After all armhole decreases have been worked, bind off rem 30 (32, 34) sts for back neck.

## make the sleeves

▓ With Onyx and size 7 (4.5mm) needles, cast on 42 sts. Work in k1, p1 rib for 5 rows. Purl next row on WS, and cont in St st, inc 1 st each side every 8th (6th, 6th) row 8 (2, 8) times, every 10th (8th, 8th) row 5 (13, 9) times—68 (72, 78) sts. Work even until piece measures 18 (18½, 19)"/45.5 (47, 48)cm from beg.

## shape the raglan cap

▓ Work same as back raglan armhole shaping. Bind off rem 12 sts.

## finishing

▓ Block pieces to measurements. If desired, work strings in Duplicate st. Sew raglan sleeve caps to raglan armholes. Sew side and sleeve seams. With crochet hook and Onyx, work 1 round of single crochet edge evenly around neck opening.

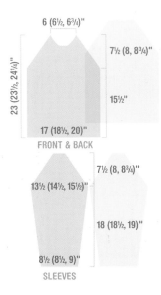

6 (6½, 6¾)"

7½ (8, 8¾)"

23 (23½, 24¼)"

15½"

17 (18½, 20)"

FRONT & BACK

7½ (8, 8¾)"

13½ (14½, 15½)"

18 (18½, 19)"

8½ (8½, 9)"

SLEEVES

Getting a little tired of doing everything on the straight and narrow? We're going to throw you a curve here with an introduction to knitting in the round.

# Knitting in the
## Round

This means instead of working back and forth as you do with straight needles, you simply keep knitting (or purling) in a spiral of sorts, creating a tube rather than a flat piece of knitting. To do this you are going to need those circular needles we discussed way back in Chapter 1.

**Circulars** can be found in several lengths. You'll need to choose one that is long enough to hold all of your stitches, but short enough so the stitches are not stretched when joined.

(Don't stress too much about this—your pattern instructions will tell you how long the needles need to be.) Cast on your stitches just as you would for straight knitting, taking care not to twist the stitches. (If you do, your fabric will end up twisted, too.)

The last stitch you cast on will be the last stitch in your round. Place a marker over the needle so you'll know where the round ends, and start knitting as shown below:

If the plastic or nylon cord connecting your circular needles gets curled, immerse it in hot water to work out the kinks.

**1.** Hold the needle tip with the cast-on stitch in your right hand and the tip with the first cast-on stitch in your left hand. Knit the first cast-on stitch, pulling the yarn tight to avoid a gap.

**2.** Work until you reach the marker. This completes the first round. Slip the marker to the right needle and work the next round.

As you join rounds, make sure the stitches are not twisted. Keeping the cast-on edge facing the center will help keep things straight.

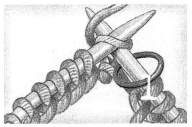

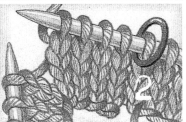

Knitting with five needles may feel awkward at first, but once you've gotten the hang of it, knitting socks can be addictive. These pedicure socks feature self-striping yarn, ribbing and a surprise toe-flap.

## materials

1 ball in #200 Jelly Bean Stripe of Magic Stripes by Lion Brand, 3½oz/100g ball, approx 330yd/300m (wool/nylon)
One set (5) size 4 (3.5mm) double-pointed needles (dpns) OR SIZE TO OBTAIN GAUGE
Size D/3 (3.25mm) crochet hook
Two ½"/13mm buttons

## finished measurements

Sized for women's shoe size 7–8 (39/40).
Approx 8"/20.5cm wide at top edge and foot is approx 9¾"/24.5cm long

## the gauge

30 sts and 32 rows to 4"/10cm over rib pat using size 4 (3.5mm) dpns (slightly stretched).
BE SURE TO GET THE GAUGE.

## make the sock

■ Cast on 60 sts loosely. Divide sts among 4 needles—15 sts on each needle. The space between needles #1 and #4 is the center of the sock. Join, taking care not to twist sts on needles. Work around in k2, p1 rib for 12"/30.5cm.

## make the heel flap

■ Using spare needle, k across sts from needle #4, then needle #1—30 sts; leave sts on needles #2 and #3 unworked. Work back and forth as folls: **Row 1 (RS)** *Sl 1, k1; rep from * to end. **Row 2** *Sl 1, p1; rep from * to end. Rep these 2 rows 9 times more.

## turn the heel

■ Cont to work back and forth in short rows as folls: K20, SKP, turn, *sl 1, p10, p2 tog, turn, sl 1, k10, SKP, turn; rep from * until all sts have been worked—12 sts on needle. **Next row (RS)** K6 sts onto needle #4, then k 6 sts onto needle #1.

## form the gussets

■ Using needle #1, pick up and k 15 sts evenly spaced along edge of heel. Cont to work in the rnd, work in rib pat on needles #2 and #3. Using the spare needle, pick up and k 15 sts evenly spaced along edge of heel, then k 6 sts from needle #4—21 sts on needles #1 and #4.

## shape the instep

■ **Rnd 1** Needle #1—SKP, k to end. Needle #2—Work in rib pat. Needle #3—Work in rib pat. Needle #4—K to last 2 sts, k2tog. **Rnds 2 and 3** Needle #1—Knit. Needle #2—Work in rib pat. Needle #3—Work in rib pat. Needle #4—Knit. Rep rnds 1–3 until there are 15 sts on needles #1 and #4—60 sts.

## make the foot

■ Keeping sts on needles #1 and #4 in St st and rem sts in rib pat, work even until foot measures 8"/20.5cm from end of heel.

## make the toe flap

■ **Next rnd** (toe opening) Needle #1—Knit. Needle #2—Knit. Needle #3—Knit. Needle #4—Bind off 15 sts. Needle #1—Bind off 15 sts—30 sts. Transfer sts from needle #3 to end of needle #2.

## shape the toe flap

Work back and forth in rows as foll:

■ **Dec row (RS)** K1, SKP, k to last 3 sts, k2tog, k1. Purl next row. Rep last 2 rows 7 times more—14 sts.

■ **Inc row 1 (RS)** K1, M1, k to last st, M1, k1. Purl next row. Rep last 2 rows 5 times more—26 sts.

■ **Inc row 2** K1, M1, [k1, p1] 12 times, M1, p1—28 sts.

■ **Next row** [K1, p1] 14 times.

■ **Inc row 3** K1, M1, [k1, p1] 14 times, M1, p1—30 sts.

■ **Next row** [K1, p1] 15 times. Bind off all sts loosely in rib.

## finish the sock

■ Sew side seams of toe flap.

## make the button loop

■ With crochet hook, ch 5. Fasten off. Sew button loop to center of toe. Position botton on center top of foot and 3¾"/9.5cm from tip of toe; sew in place.

1

This classic watch cap is knit in the round, with yarn, color and texture variations to alter the look. Choose from the three versions presented here or create an original all your own.

## materials

**Version #1:** 1 skein in #321 Williamsburg of Homespun® by Lion Brand, 6oz/170g skein, approx 185yd/169m (polyester)

Size 9 (5.5mm) 16"/40cm long circular and double pointed needles (dpns).

**Version #2:** 1 skein each in #126 Coffee and #125 Mocha of Lion Suede by Lion Brand, 3oz/85g skein, each approx 122yd/110m (polyester/acrylic)

Size 8 (5mm) 16"/40cm circular and double pointed needles

**Version #3:** 1 skein each in #302 Colonial and #378 Olive Homespun® by Lion Brand, 6oz/170g skein, each approx 185yd/169m (acrylic/polyester)

Size 10 (6mm) 16"/40cm circular and double pointed needles

Stitch marker

## finished measurements

**Circumference** 21"/53.5cm (unstretched)

**Length** 10"/25.5cm

## the gauge

15 sts and 19 rows to 4"/10cm over k2, p2 rib using size 10 (6mm) needles. BE SURE TO GET THE GAUGE.

## make the hat version #1

■ With circular needle, cast on 60 sts. Join, taking care not to twist sts on needle. Place a marker for beg of rnd and slip marker every rnd.

**Rnds 1–8** Work even in St st. **Rnd 9** *K2, p2; rep from * around. Repeat last rnd until piece measures 7½"/19cm from beg. **Note** Transfer sts to dpn at this point or when number of sts becomes too small to work with circular needle. **Next rnd** *K1, ssk, p1; rep from * around—45 sts.

**Next rnd** *K2, p1; rep from * around. Rep last rnd until piece measures 10"/25.5cm from beg. **Last rnd** *K1, ssk; rep from * around—30 sts.

■ Bind off all sts. Cut a 12"/30.5cm tail, weave tail through top and draw together. Weave in ends.

## make the hat version #2

■ Work as for Version #1 with color changes as follows:

Beg with Coffee, work through Rnd 8. Change to Mocha and work 2 rnds. Alternate 2 rnds Coffee and 2 rnds Mocha for remainder of cap.

## make the hat version #3

■ Work as for Version #1, beg with Colonial and cont alternating 2 rnds Olive and 2 rnds Colonial for 14 rnds. Finish remainder of cap in Colonial.

# Sizing and Construction

## Size matters

Knitting a garment can take weeks or even months to complete, so the last thing you want to discover is that the garment is two sizes too large (or worse, too small). Make sure you are happy with the fit of your project by paying close attention to the measurements given in the pattern. To size yourself up against the pattern, stand in your undies and measure around the fullest part of your chest. If you are knitting a skirt, shorts or dress, you'll also need to measure around your hips (at the widest part) and natural waistline (to find this, tie a piece of string around your middle and see where it falls). As you measure, hold the tape snug, but not tight—and don't cheat. Giving yourself a few inches more or less may help your ego, but it won't get you a garment that fits properly. Compare the bust/chest measurement in the pattern to your own measurements, remembering that the numbers given in the pattern refer to the finished size of the garment, not the goods hidden under it. Choose the size with the bust (for sweaters) or hip (for skirts) measurement that comes closest to your own. (Choose dresses by bust size, as it is easier to alter at the hips if you need to.) You may want to measure a sweater you like that is similar in style to the one shown in the pattern and use it as a guide for picking your size.

## The scheme of things

Toward the end of many sweater patterns you'll find a mini representation of the sweater's pieces, called a schematic. Drawn to scale, these little line illustrations are labeled with the name (back, sleeve, left front, etc.) and the exact measurements of the piece. They also allow you to see the shape of the item you are about to make. If you've followed the instructions correctly, your knit pieces will look just like the picture when you've finished. Here's what your average schematic for a simple sweater looks like.

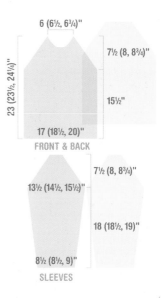

6 (6½, 6¾)"

7½ (8, 8¾)"

23 (23½, 24¼)"

15½"

17 (18½, 20)"

FRONT & BACK

13½ (14½, 15½)"

7½ (8, 8¾)"

18 (18½, 19)"

8½ (8½, 9)"

SLEEVES

The numbers preceding the parentheses represent the measurements for the smallest size; those inside indicate measurements for sequentially increasing sizes. For a cardigan, the schematic will usually show just one of the two fronts, and you'll have to imagine a mirror image for the other. (We can't do everything for you, you know.)

## Measuring up

You should also use the schematic to make sure the measurements of your finished knit pieces match those given in the pattern instructions. To see how your pieces are shaping up as you knit, lay the piece out on a flat, smooth surface and, using a tape measure, take the measurement in the middle of a row. Determine the length of your work by measuring from the row below your needle to the bottom edge. When measuring the length of an armhole, don't measure along the curve or slanted edge—if you do the measurement will be inaccurate. Instead, measure in a straight line from the needle to the first armhole decrease.

## Block parties

Before you're ready to stitch your sweater together you'll need to block (which is just a knitty way of saying wet, pin and steam) the pieces into shape. Like the dreaded gauge swatch, this is one rather tedious step that is tempting to skip. DON'T. Blocking is to knitting as steaming is to sewing. Without it, your perfectly knit project will look sloppy and homemade—and not in a good way.

## pressing guide

Because fibers react differently to heat, it is best to know what to expect before you press or steam them. Just remember that there are many combinations of fibers, and you should choose a process that is compatible with all the components of your yarn. If you are unsure about the fiber content of your yarn, test your gauge swatch before blocking your sweater pieces.

| | |
|---|---|
| Angora | Wet block by spraying. |
| Cotton | Wet block or warm/hot steam press. |
| Linen | Wet block or warm/hot steam press. |
| Lurex | Do not block. |
| Mohair | Wet block by spraying. |
| Novelties | Do not block. |
| Synthetics | Carefully follow instructions on ball band—usually wet block by spraying. Do not press. |
| Wool and all wool-like fibers (alpaca, camel hair, cashmere) | Wet block by spraying or warm steam press. |
| Wool blends | Wet block by spraying. Do not press unless tested. |

There are two kinds of blocking: wet and steam. To determine which you should use with your yarn, check out our handy pressing guide (below).

For **wet blocking**, immerse the pieces in cool water, squeeze them out, stretch them on an ironing board or pressing pad (a folded towel will also do) and pin them to their exact measurements, or pin first and use a spray bottle to dampen the fabric. Then leave 'em alone until they are completely dry. For **steam blocking**, pin the pieces to their measurements on your board, then fire up your iron to steam. Hold the iron close to the fabric (don't actually touch the pieces with the iron) and steam away until everything is nice and damp. As with wet blocking, you'll leave the pieces to dry.

## Just sew

Okay, so you have all the pieces for your sweater finished and blocked to perfect size. It's time to put them together to create the garment (or bag, or whatever else you are making).

Things will go easier if you assemble the pieces as follows: **1.** Connect the shoulders. **2.** Finish the neck edge (the pattern instructions will tell you how to do this). **3.** Sew the sleeves to the body of the sweater. **4.** Sew continually from the end of the sleeve to the underarm and then down the body of the sweater to the bottom edge. Our handy sweater map shows you how it all fits together and explains what you need to do to prepare each piece. Nice, huh?

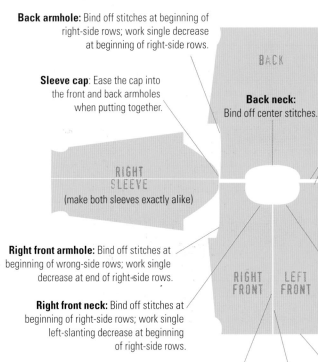

**Back armhole:** Bind off stitches at beginning of right-side rows; work single decrease at beginning of right-side rows.

**Back armhole:** Bind off stitches at beginning of wrong-side rows; work single decrease at end of right-side rows.

**Sleeve cap:** Ease the cap into the front and back armholes when putting together.

**Shoulders:** Seam the front and back shoulders together either by sewing the bound-off stitches together, or use the Three-Needle Bind-off.

**Back neck:** Bind off center stitches.

BACK

RIGHT SLEEVE
(make both sleeves exactly alike)

LEFT SLEEVE

**Right front armhole:** Bind off stitches at beginning of wrong-side rows; work single decrease at end of right-side rows.

**Left front armhole:** Bind off stitches a beginning of right-side rows; work sing decrease at beginning of right-side row

**Right front neck:** Bind off stitches at beginning of right-side rows; work single left-slanting decrease at beginning of right-side rows.

RIGHT FRONT    LEFT FRONT

**Left front neck:** Bind off stitches at beginning of wrong-side rows; work single right-slant decrease at end of right-side rows.

**Ribbing:** Usually worked with smaller size needles.

**Buttonhole band (for women):** Pick up stitches along the right front edge, and work buttonholes in the center of the band to correspond to button markers.

**Button band (for women):** Make this edge first by picking up stitches along the left front edge to work the band and mark placement of the buttons.

To actually join the pieces together, you're going to need a needle and thread. Line up the pieces by finding the cast-on stitches on both sides. Use pins to hold them together. Next, count up about 10 rows on each side and pin the corresponding stitches together. Keep at it until you reach the tops of the two pieces. On projects worked all in one piece (a hat or tube top, for instance), the rows should line up exactly. If they don't, go back and see where you slipped up. When you are pinning two separate pieces (a sweater back and front, for example) you may have to ease in extra rows if one piece is slightly longer than the other.

Once you have everything pinned, you can begin seaming using one of the following methods.

## How to begin seaming

If you have a long tail left from your cast-on row, you can use this strand to begin sewing. To make a neat join at the lower edge with no gap, use the technique shown here.

1. Thread the strand into a yarn needle. With the right sides of both pieces facing you, insert the yarn needle from back to front into the corner stitch of the piece without the tail. Making a figure eight with the yarn, insert the needle from back to front into the stitch with the cast-on tail. Tighten to close the gap.

## Vertical seam on stockinette stitch

2. The vertical seam is worked from the right side and is used to join two edges row by row. It hides the uneven stitches at the edge of a row and creates an invisible seam, making the knitting appear continuous.

Insert the yarn needle under the horizontal bar between the first and second stitches. Insert the needle into the corresponding bar on the other piece. Continue alternating from side to side.

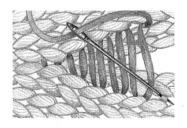

## Vertical seam on ribbing

**Purl to purl**

3. When joining ribbing with a purl stitch at each edge, insert the yarn needle under the horizontal bar in the center of a knit stitch on each side in order to keep the pattern continuous.

**Knit to knit**

**4.** When joining ribbing with a knit stitch at each edge, use the bottom loop of the purl stitch on one side and the top loop of the corresponding purl stitch on the other side.

**Purl to knit**

**5.** When joining purl and knit stitch edges, skip knit stitch and join two purl stitches as shown.

## Vertical seam on garter stitch

This seam joins two edges row by row, like vertical seaming on stockinette stitch. The alternating pattern of catching top and bottom loops of the stitches ensures that only you can tell there's a join.

**6.** Insert the yarn needle into the top loop on one side, then in the bottom loop of the corresponding stitch on the other side. Continue to alternate in this way.

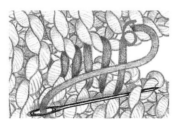

## Horizontal seam on stockinette stitch

**7.** This seam is used to join two bound-off edges, as for shoulder seams or hoods, and is worked stitch by stitch. Each piece must have the same number of stitches so that the finished seam will resemble a continuous row of knit stitches. Be sure to pull the yarn tightly enough to hide the bound-off edges.

With the bound-off edges together, and lined up stitch for stitch, insert the yarn needle under a stitch inside the bound-off edge of one side and then under the corresponding stitch on the other side. Repeat all the way across the join.

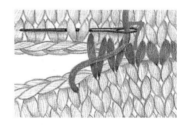

## Vertical to horizontal seam

**8.** Used to connect a bound-off edge to a vertical length of knitted fabric, this seam requires careful pre-measuring and marking to ensure an even seam. Insert the yarn needle under a stitch inside the bound-off edge of the vertical piece.

Insert the needle under one or two horizontal bars between the first and second stitches of

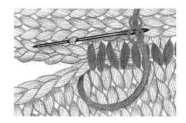

the horizontal piece. (shown opposite on stockinette stitch).

## Slip-stitch crochet seam

**1.** This method creates a visible, though very strong, seam. Use it when you don't mind a bulky join or are looking for an especially sturdy connection.

With the right sides together, insert the crochet hook through both thicknesses. Catch the yarn and draw a loop through. *Insert the hook again. Draw a loop through both thicknesses and the loop on the hook. Repeat from *, keeping the stitches straight and even.

## Backstitch

**2.** The backstitch creates a strong, neat, bulky seam that's perfect for extra reinforcement. With the right sides of the pieces facing each other, secure the seam by taking the needle twice around the edges from back to front. Bring the needle up about ¼"/5mm from where the yarn last emerged, as shown.

**3.** In one motion, insert the needle into the point where the yarn emerged from the previous stitch and back up approximately ¼"/5mm ahead of the emerging yarn. Pull the yarn through. Repeat this step, keeping the stitches straight and even.

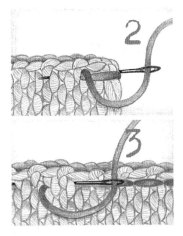

Knitting in garter stitch in the round with
multiple strands of yarn yields a fast, fancy
carryall. Purchased handles add to the quick
finish.

## materials

2 balls in #146 Fuchsia (MC) of Lion Cotton by Lion Brand, 5oz/140g balls, each
approx 236yd/212m (cotton)

1 ball in #210 Rainbow (CC) of Fun Fur Prints by Lion Brand, 1½oz/40g ball, approx
57yd/52m (polyester)

One pair size 9 (5.5mm) needles OR SIZE TO OBTAIN GAUGE

Size 9 (5.5mm) circular needle, 16"/40cm long

One pair 6"/15cm natural cane round handbag handles

Stitch markers

## finished measurements

Approx 14"/35.5cm wide,10"/25.5cm high and 2½"/6.5cm deep (excluding handles)

## the gauge

15 sts and 21 rows to 4"/10cm over pat st using 2 strands of MC held tog and size 9
(5.5mm) needles. BE SURE TO GET THE GAUGE.

**Notes**

Use 2 strands of MC held tog throughout.

Use 3 strands of CC held tog throughout.

Body of bag is worked in the round, then top shaping and openings for handles are
worked back and forth in rows.

Bottom gusset is worked back and forth in rows.

**Pattern stitch I**

**On circular needle**

■ **Rnd 1** Knit. **Rnd 2** Purl. **Rnds 3 and 4** Knit. Rep rnds 1–4 for pat st I.

**Pattern stitch II**

**On straight needles**

■ **Rows 1–3** Knit. **Row 4** Purl. Rep rows 1–4 for pat st II.

## make the body

With circular needle and 2 strands of MC held tog, cast on 38 sts, pm to indicate side edge of bag, cast on another 38 sts—76 sts. Join and pm to indicate opposite-side edge of bag. Work in pat st I for 4 rnds. **Inc rnd** K to first marker, M1, sl marker, k to 2nd marker, M1, sl marker—78 sts. Beg with rnd 2, work 3 rnds even. Rep last 4 rnds 8 times more—94 sts. Rep inc rnd on next rnd, then every 3rd rnd 5 times more—106 sts. Knit next rnd.

## shape the top and the openings for the handles

Change to straight needles. For front of bag, work as folls: **Row 1 (RS)** K23, place these sts on holder for upper right top, bind off next 7 sts, k23 (this brings you to 2nd marker); leave rem sts on circular needle for back of bag. Turn.

## shape the upper left top

**Row 2** Bind off first 2 sts purlwise, p to last 2 sts, p2tog—20 sts. **Row 3** K2tog, k to end—19 sts. **Row 4** Bind off first 2 sts knitwise, k to end—17 sts. **Row 5** K2tog, k to end—16 sts. **Row 6** Bind off first 2 sts purlwise, p to end—14 sts. **Row 7** K2tog, k to end—13 sts. **Row 8** Bind off first 2 sts knitwise, k to end—11 sts. **Row 9** K2tog, k to end—10 sts. **Row 10** Bind off first 2 sts purlwise, p to end—8 sts. **Row 11** K2tog, k to end—7 sts. **Row 12** Bind off first 2 sts knitwise, k to end—5 sts. **Row 13** K2tog, k to end—4 sts. **Row 14** Bind off first 2 sts purlwise, p to end—2 sts. **Row 15** K2tog. Fasten off last st. Place sts on holder back to LH needle ready for a WS row.

## shape the upper right top

**Row 2 (WS)** P2tog, p to end—22 sts. **Row 3** Bind off first 2 sts knitwise, k to last 2 sts, k2tog—19 sts. **Row 4** K2tog, k to end—18 sts. **Row 5** Bind off first 2 sts knitwise, k to end—16 sts. **Row 6** P2tog, p to end—15 sts. **Row 7** Bind off first 2 sts knitwise, k to end—13 sts. **Row 8** K2tog, k to end—12 sts. **Row 9** Bind off first 2 sts knitwise, k to end—10 sts. **Row 10** P2tog, p to end—9 sts. **Row 11** Bind off first 2 sts knitwise, k to end—7 sts. **Row 12** K2tog, k to end—6 sts. **Row 13** Bind off first 2 sts knitwise, k to last 2 sts, k2tog—3 sts. **Row 14** P2tog, p1—2 sts. **Row 15** K2tog. Fasten off last st.
For back of bag, work as folls: **Row 1 (RS)** K23 sts from circular needle, place these sts on holder for upper right top, bind off next 7 sts, k23. Turn. Cont to work upper left top, then upper right top as for front of bag.

## make the bottom gusset

With straight needles and 2 strands of MC held tog, cast on 4 sts. **Rows 1 and 2** Knit. **Row 3** K2, M1, k2—5 sts. **Row 4** Purl. **Row 5** K2, M1, k1, M1, k2—7 sts. **Rows 6 and 7** Knit. **Row 8** Purl. **Row 9** K2, M1, k3, M1, k2—9 sts. **Row 10** Knit. **Row 11** K4, M1, k5—10 sts. **Row 12** Purl. **Rows 13–15** Knit. **Row 16** Purl. **Row 17** K4, M1, k2, M1, k4—12 sts. **Rows 18–35** Beg with row 2, work even in pat st II for 18 rows, end on row 3. **Row 36** K1, k2tog, k6, k2tog, k1—10 sts. **Row 37** Purl. **Rows 38–40** Knit. **Row 41** Purl. **Row 42** K4, k2tog, k4—9 sts. **Rows 43 and 44** Knit. **Row 45** Purl. **Row 46** K2, k2tog, k1, k2tog, k2—7 sts. **Rows 47 and 48** Knit. **Row 49** Purl. **Row 50** [K1, k2tog] twice, k1—5 sts. **Row 51** Knit. **Row 52** K1, k2tog, k1—4 sts. Bind off.

## finish the bag

Sew bottom gusset to bottom opening in bag.
Add the trim. With RS facing, straight needles and 3 strands of CC held tog, pick up and k 40 sts evenly spaced along top edge of one side between shaping for front and back handles. Knit 1 row. Bind off all sts knitwise. Rep on opposite top edge of bag. Using 2 strands of MC, whipstitch handles in place.

Most of the styles we've shown you have what are called self-finishing edges, meaning that your cast-on or bind-off row serves as the edge of your neckline, cuff or hem. But for some projects you'll need to take things a step further, picking up stitches to add a collar, cuff, button band or border. And, of course, if you are adding a button band, you are going to need some buttonholes to go with it. Let see how it's all done, shall we?

# Pick-Me-Ups

**Picking up stitches** simply means that you'll use a needle or crochet hook to dip a new strand of yarn in and out of the edge of your knitting fabric, creating new loops to serve as the foundation row for your collar, button band or whatever else the pattern calls for. It's very easy to do, as long as you keep two things in mind: 1. Make sure you start picking up with the right side facing out, and 2. Space those new stitches evenly across the fabric. Here's how it's done:

## Picking up on vertical edge with knitting needle

1. Insert the knitting needle into the corner stitch of the first row, one stitch in from the side edge. Wrap the yarn around the needle knitwise.

2. Draw the yarn through. You have picked up one stitch. Continue to pick up stitches along the edge. Occasionally skip one row to keep the edge from flaring.

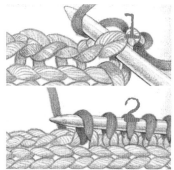

## Picking up on horizontal edge with crochet hook

1. Insert the crochet hook from front to back into the center of the first stitch one row below the bound-off edge. Catch the yarn and pull a loop through.

2. Slip the loop onto the knitting needle, being sure it is not twisted. Continue to pick up one stitch in each stitch along the bound-off edge.

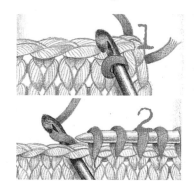

# Let's Neck

When you pick up stitches on a curved edge (necklines are a good example) you'll have to be even more careful with the spacing and number of stitches you pick up. Too many and the band will flare out, too few and it will pull in. We explain below:

## Marking edge for picking up stitches

Stitches must be picked up evenly so that the band will not flare or pull in. Place pins, markers or yarn, as shown above, every 2"/5cm, and pick up the same number of stitches between each pair of markers. If you know the number of stitches to be picked up, divide this by the number of sections to determine how many stitches to pick up in each one. If you don't have a final count, use the marked sections to ensure even spacing around the neck.

## Picking up stitches along a shaped edge

Pick up stitches neatly just inside the shaped edge, following the curve and hiding the jagged selvage.

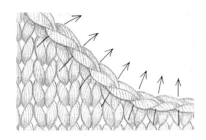

## Picking up stitches along a diagonal edge

Pick up stitches one stitch in from the shaped edge, keeping them in a straight line.

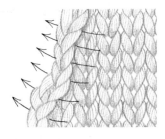

# here's how

If your coat or cardigan will close with **buttons**, you're going to need a few openings to slip them through. Start by placing **markers** (you can use pins or little pieces of yarn) on the button band for the first and last buttonhole, then measure the distance between and space the remaining markers accordingly. Got that done? Good. Now let's move on to creating the **buttonholes** themselves.

We're going to show you two of the easiest techniques for picture-perfect buttonholes, starting with the most common, the **two-row horizontal** style. This one is nice because you can easily make it larger or smaller. To create it, you simply bind off a number of stitches on one row, then cast them on again on the next, like so:

1. On the first row, work to the placement of the buttonhole. Knit two; with the left needle, pull one stitch over the other stitch, *knit one, pull the second stitch over the knit one; repeat from the * twice more. Four stitches have been bound off.

2. On the next row, work to the bound-off stitches and cast on four stitches. On the next row, work these stitches through the back loops to tighten them.

## two-row horizontal buttonhole

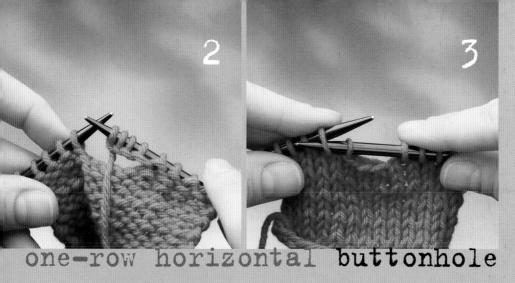

# one-row horizontal buttonhole

Slightly more difficult to execute is the **one-row horizontal** buttonhole. But since it's nice, neat, and very sturdy we think it's worth the extra effort.

1. Work to the buttonhole, bring yarn to front and slip a stitch purlwise. Place yarn at back and leave it there. *Slip next stitch from left needle. Pass the first slipped stitch over it; repeat from the * three times more (not moving yarn). Slip the last bound-off stitch to left needle and turn work.

2. Cast on five stitches as follows, using cable cast-on with the yarn at the back:

*Insert the right needle between the first and second stitches on the left needle, draw up a loop, place the loop on the left needle; repeat from the * four times more, turn the work.

3. Slip the first stitch with the yarn in back from the left needle and pass the extra cast-on stitch over it to close the buttonhole. Work to the end of the row.

# Button Up

Once your buttonhole is in place, you can sew on the buttons. To get the holes and the buttons to line up correctly, **count** the number of rows between the lower edge and the first buttonhole, between the first and second hole, and so on. Then place markers for buttons on the corresponding rows of the **button band**.

Use yarn or matching thread and a tapestry needle to **stitch** the buttons in place. Double the yarn and knot the ends, then slip your button onto the needle and stitch it to the fabric.

Details prevail in this stylish cardigan designed by Joan Forgione. Worked in several panels and accented with dramatic ribbing and buttons, it features a cropped waist and unusual front button band shaping.

## materials

6 (6, 7, 8, 9) balls in #175 Green of Wool-Ease® by Lion Brand, 3oz/85g balls, each approx 197yd/180m (acrylic/wool)

One pair size 6 and 8 (4 and 5 mm) needles OR SIZE TO OBTAIN GAUGE

Three 1½"/38mm buttons

Sized for X-Small (Small, Medium, Large, X-Large). Shown in size Small.

## the measurements

**Bust** 34¼ (36½, 39½, 42¾, 46)"/87 (92.5, 100, 108.5, 116.5)cm

**Length** 18 (18½, 19½, 20, 21)"/46 (47, 49.5, 50.5, 53.5)cm

**Upper arm** 13¼ (14¼, 15, 16, 17)"/33.5 (37, 38, 40.5, 43)cm

## the gauges

■ 18 sts and 24 rows to 4"/10cm over St st using larger needles.

■ 24 sts and 30 rows to 4"/10cm over k3, p3 rib using smaller needles.

BE SURE TO GET THE GAUGES.

## note

■ Body of cardigan is worked in 5 pieces: back, fronts and side panels.

K3, p3 rib (multiple of 6 sts plus 5) **Row 1 (RS)** K1 (selvage st), k3, *p3, k3; rep from *, end k1 (selvage st).

**Row 2** K1, k the knit sts and p the purl sts to last st, k1. Rep row 2 for k3, p3 rib.

## make the back

■ With smaller needles, cast on 83 (95, 101, 113, 119) sts. Work in k3, p3 rib, dec 1 st each side (inside of selvage sts) every 4th row 6 times—71 (83, 89, 101, 107) sts, ending with a WS row. Change to larger needles. K next row on RS, dec 17 (23, 23, 25, 25) sts evenly across row—54 (60, 66, 76, 82) sts. Cont in St st for 2½ (2½, 2½, 3½, 3½)"/6.5 (6.5, 6.5, 9, 9)cm, ending with a WS row.

■ Inc 1 st each side (inside of selvage sts) on next row, then every 4th row 4 (4, 4, 3, 4) times more—64 (70, 76, 84, 92) sts. Work evenly until piece measures 10 (10, 10½, 10½, 11)"/25.5 (25.5, 26.5, 26.5, 28)cm from beg.

## shape the armhole

■ Bind off 2 sts at beg of next 2 (2, 4, 4, 4) rows, dec 1 st each side every other row 2 (2, 1, 2, 3) times—56 (62, 66, 72, 78) sts. Work even until armhole measures 5½ (6, 6½, 7, 7½)"/14 (15, 16.5, 18, 19)cm, end with a WS row.

## shape the neck

■ **Next row (RS)** Work 21 (24, 26, 29, 32) sts, join 2nd ball of yarn and bind off center 14 sts, knit to end. Change to smaller needles. **Next (inc) row (WS)** Working in k3, p3 rib, inc 5 (8, 8, 9, 9) sts evenly across sts on each side—26 (32, 34, 38, 41) sts. Cont in rib, bind off from each neck edge 4 sts once, 3 sts once and 2 sts once and 1 st once—16 (22, 24, 28, 31) sts each side. Work even, if necessary, until armhole measures 7 (7½, 8, 8½, 9)"/18 (19, 20.5, 21.5, 23)cm.

## shape the shoulders

■ Bind off from each shoulder edge 5 (7, 8, 9, 10) sts twice, 6 (8, 8, 10, 11) sts once.

## make the left front

■ With smaller needles, cast on 34 (40, 43, 49, 52) sts. Work in k3, p3 rib as foll: **Row 1 (RS)** K1 (selvage st), p3 (3, 0, 0, 3), *k3, p3; rep from * to end. Cont in rib as established, dec 1 st at side edge (beg of RS rows and inside of selvage st) every 4th row 6 times—28 (34, 37, 43, 46) sts, ending with a WS row. Change to larger needles. K next row on RS, dec 6 (10, 10, 11, 12) sts evenly across—22 (24, 27, 32, 34) sts. Cont in St st for 2½ (2½, 2½, 3½, 3½)"/6.5 (6.5, 6.5, 9, 9)cm, ending with a WS row.

■ Inc 1 st at side edge only same as back—27 (29, 32, 36, 39) sts. Work even until piece measures same length as back to armhole.

## shape the armhole

■ Shape armhole at side edge (beg of RS rows) as for back—23 (25, 27, 30, 32) sts. Work even until armhole measures 5 (5½, 6, 6½, 7)"/12.5 (14, 15, 16.5, 18)cm, ending with a RS row.

## shape the neck and shoulder

■ **Next row (WS)** Bind off 3 sts (neck edge), work to end. Cont to bind off from neck edge 3 sts 2 (1, 1, 1, 0) times mores, 2 sts 0 (1, 1, 1, 2) times—14 (17, 19, 22, 25) sts. Work 1 row even on RS. Change to smaller needles. **Next (inc) row (WS)** Working in k3, p3 rib, inc 5 (8, 8, 9, 9) sts evenly across row—19 (25, 27, 31, 34) sts. Dec 1 st at neck edge every other row 3 times—16 (22, 24, 28, 31) sts. Work even until armhole measures same as back to shoulder. Shape shoulder at side edge as for back.

## make the right front

■ Work to correspond to left front, reversing all shaping.

## make the side panels

■ **Note** Side panels do not have selvage sts. With smaller needles, cast on 60 (60, 63, 63, 66) sts. Work in k3, p3 rib as foll: K0 (0, 3, 3, 0), *p3, k3; rep from * to end. Cont in rib for 3"/7.5cm. Bind off all sts.

## make the sleeves

■ With smaller needles, cast on 62 (62, 68, 68, 68) sts. Work in k3, p3 rib as foll: K1 (selvage st), *k3, p3; rep from *, end k1 (selvage st). Cont in rib as established for 3"/7.5cm, ending with a WS row. K next row on RS for turning ridge for sleeve cuff. **Next row** Reverse k3, p3 rib so that sleeve matches when cuff is turned back and work in k3, p3 rib for an additional 3"/7.5cm, ending with a RS row. Change to larger needles. P next row on WS, dec 14 (14, 16, 16, 14) sts evenly across row—48 (48, 52, 52, 54) sts. Cont in St st, inc 1 st each side (inside of selvage sts) every 8th (6th, 6th, 4th, 4th) row 3 (5, 5, 3, 6) times, every 10th (8th, 8th, 6th, 6th) row 3 (3, 3, 7, 5) times—60 (64, 68, 72, 76) sts. Work evenly until sleeve measures 16"/40.5cm from beg.

## shape the sleeve cap

■ Bind off 7 sts at beg of next 2 rows, 2 sts at beg of next 2 (2, 4, 4, 4) rows, 1 st at beg of next 8 (8, 10, 10, 12) rows. *Bind off 2 sts at beg of next 2 rows. Work 2 rows even.* Rep between *s twice more. Bind off 2 sts at beg of next 4 (6, 4, 6, 6) rows. Bind off rem 14 (14, 16, 16, 18) sts.

## finish the cardigan

■ Sew shoulder seams. Sew side panels to front and back. Sew sleeve seams. Sew sleeves to body of sweater.

## make the neckband

■ With smaller needles and RS facing, beg at right front buttonhole band and pick up and knit 95 sts evenly around neck opening. **Next row (WS)** K1 (selvage), work in k3, p3 rib to last stitch, k1 (selvage). Work in k3, p3 rib pattern as established for 6 rows, binding off 1 st at beg of each row. Bind off rem 89 sts loosely.

## make the button band

■ With RS facing and smaller needles, beg at top of left front neckband, pick up and k 99 (105, 105, 117, 117) sts along left front edge. Work in k3, p3 for 1¼"/3cm, ending with a RS row. Bind off 30 sts at beg of next WS row. Cont in rib until band measures 3"/7.5cm. Bind off in rib. Place markers on band for 3 buttons, the first and last ones 1½"/4cm from each edge and one centered in between.

## make the buttonhole band

■ Work as for button band, working buttonholes opposite markers after band measures 1¼"/3cm as foll: Work to marker, work on these sts only for 4 rows. *Cut yarn. Join new yarn and work to next marker. Work on these sts only for 4 rows; rep from * twice more. On next row, rib across all sts and complete as for button band.

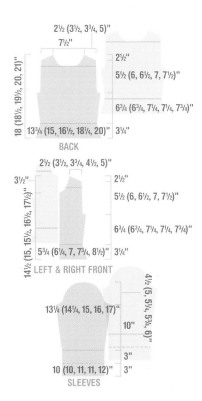

2½ (3½, 3¾, 5)"

7½"

2½"

5½ (6, 6½, 7, 7½)"

6¾ (6¾, 7¼, 7¼, 7¾)"

18 (18¼, 19½, 20, 21)"

13¾ (15, 16½, 18¼, 20)"  3¼"

BACK

2½ (3½, 3¾, 4½, 5)"

3½"

2½"

5½ (6, 6½, 7, 7½)"

6¾ (6¾, 7¼, 7¼, 7¾)"

14½ (15, 15½, 16½, 17½)"

5¾ (6¼, 7, 7¾, 8½)"  3¼"

LEFT & RIGHT FRONT

4½ (5, 5¼, 5¾, 6)"

13¼ (14¼, 15, 16, 17)"

10"

3"

10 (10, 11, 11, 12)"  3"

SLEEVES

At first glance, knitting instructions may seem like they are written in some sort of secret code. They're not. It's just that to save space and make directions a bit clearer, those who write patterns have come up with a few shorthand ways to get the point across. The glossary below should get you through just about any project. We've also included a handy list of U.S. knitting needle sizes and their metric equivalents.

**approx** approximately

**beg** begin, beginning

**cont** continue

**dec** decrease

**foll** follow(s)

**in/cm/mm** inches/centimeters/millimeters

**inc** increase

**inc(dec)...sts evenly across row** Count the number of stitches in the row, and then divide that number by the number of stitches to be increased (decreased). The result of this division will tell you how many stitches to work between each increased (decreased) stitch.

**k the knit and p the purl sts** This is a phrase used when a pattern of knit and purl stitches has been established and will be continued for some time. When the stitch that's facing you looks like a V, knit it. When it looks like a bump, purl it.

**k** knit

**k2tog** knit two together (a method of decreasing explained on page 52)

**k3tog** knit three together. Worked same as k2tog, but insert needle into three sts instead of two for a double decrease.

**knitwise** Insert the needle into the stitch as if you were going to knit it.

**oz/g** ounces/grams (usually in reference to amount of yarn in a single ball)

**p** purl

**p2tog** purl two together (a method of decreasing explained on page 52)

**pat** pattern

**pm** place marker

**purlwise** Insert the needle into the stitch as if you were going to purl it.

**sk2p** Slip one, knit two together, pass slipped stitch over k2tog

**rem** remain, remains or remaining

**rep** repeat

**rep from *** Repeat the instructions after the asterisk as many times as indicated. If the directions say "rep from * to end," continue to repeat the instructions after the asterisk to the end of the row.

**rev sc** reverse single crochet

**reverse shaping** A term used for garments such as cardigans where shaping for the right and left fronts is identical, but reversed. For example, neck edge stitches that were decreased at the beginning of the row for the first piece will be decreased at the end of the row on the second. In general, follow the directions for the first piece, being sure to mirror the decreases (increases) on each side.

**rnd**  round

**RS**  right side

**sc**  single crochet

**SKP**  Slip one stitch knitwise to right-hand needle. Knit the next stitch and pass the slipped stitch over the knit stitch.

**slip**  Transfer the indicated stitches from the left to the right needle without working (knitting or purling) them.

**Small (Medium, Large)**
The most common method of displaying changes in pattern for different sizes. In general, the measurements, stitch counts, directions, etc. for the smallest size come first, followed by the increasingly larger sizes in parentheses. If there is only one number given, it applies to all of the sizes.

**ssk**  On RS, slip next two stitches knitwise. Insert tip of left needle into fronts of these two stitches and knit them together. On WS, slip one stitch, purl one stitch, then pass slip stitch over purl stitch.

**st/sts**  stitch/stitches

**St st**  stockinette stitch

**tog**  together

**work even**  Continue in the established pattern without working any increases or decreases.

**WS:**  wrong side

**yo**  yarn over

# knitting needle sizes

| U.S. | Metric | U.S. | Metric | U.S. | Metric |
|------|--------|------|--------|------|--------|
| 0 | 2mm | 7 | 4.5mm | 15 | 10mm |
| 1 | 2.25mm | 8 | 5mm | 17 | 12.75mm |
| 2 | 2.75mm | 9 | 5.5mm | 19 | 15mm |
| 3 | 3.25mm | 10 | 6mm | 35 | 19mm |
| 4 | 3.5mm | 10.5 | 6.5mm | 50 | 25.5mm |
| 5 | 3.75mm | 11 | 8mm | | |
| 6 | 4mm | 13 | 9mm | | |

Crochet has come a long way since the days of doilies and TP covers (not that we don't appreciate the kitsch value of both). New yarns have increased the creative possibilities, and rather than trying to duplicate knit style in crochet stitches, designers are now playing up crochet's own unique qualities.

# Getting a Grip

**Hooks** are the key component in crochet construction. These come in two classifications: yarn hooks, which are used for all of the projects in this book (and most of the others you'll find elsewhere), and steel hooks that are used solely with crochet thread for lacemaking and filet techniques. Both styles comprise five distinct sections: the tip and throat (the hooked end), which are used to make the stitch, the shaft, which determines the size of the hook, and the grip and handle, which are used to hold the hook.

Yarn hooks can be found in aluminum, plastic and acrylic, as well as in natural materials like wood, bamboo and bone. Some have ergonomically shaped handles and cushioned grips that make it easier and more comfortable to work. Start with the old-fashioned aluminum style, and as you gain skill and confidence,

experiment with other styles to see which you like best.

The size of the hook (in combination with the yarn used for the project) will determine the size of your stitches. On most hooks, you'll find the size stamped on the handle. In the U.S., hooks are sized by letter of the alphabet, except for the size 7 (why, we don't know—it's one of the great mysteries of life). As the letter ascends, so does the size of the hook. Steel hooks are sized by number and reverse the equation. The larger the number, the smaller the hook. The number next to the letter is the equivalent knitting needle size. Generally, the smaller hooks are used with thinner yarns and vice versa. The yarn industry has taken some of the confusion out of matching yarn to hook by setting up a standardized system of weights and categories. You can read more about it on page 9-10 (where you will find a Standard Yarn Weight chart).

The first thing you need to learn is how to hold the hook properly. Easy enough, right? So take your pick from one of these two: The knife grip is the most recommended. With the tip and throat facing you, put your thumb flat on the front of the grip and your index finger flat on the back. Now wrap your remaining fingers around the handle.

Your second choice is the pencil grip, which looks a little more elegant, but is not quite as comfortable and is prone to strain your hands. So with the caveat that this grip may cause carpal tunnel syndrome, here's how it works. Hold the hook between your thumb and index finger with the remaining fingers folded down, just as you would a pencil.

# Hold It Right There

Once you've figured out how to hold the hook, you're ready to put it together with your yarn. It all begins with a slip knot, the little loop that anchors the yarn to the hook. First, make a loop, placing one end of the yarn centered underneath the loop. (The result, if flattened, will look like a pretzel.) Next, insert the hook under the center strand and pull it up into a loop on the hook (see photo at below). Pull both yarn ends to tighten the knot on the hook.

## get your fiber (and other goodies)

The yarns you'll use for crochet are pretty much identical to those used for knitting (read all about them on page 9). Tool-wise you'll need many of the same supplies we discussed in Chapter 1 in the knitting section: small sharp scissors, a tape measure, split-ring stitch markers, a tapestry needle and a knitting gauge (you can use this to measure crochet gauge, too).

# here's how

We promise we'll get to the **fun stuff** soon, but for now, you'll have to content yourself with laying the **foundation chain** for all those groovy stitches to come. This is simply a series of **loops** (called chain stitches) that link together. Crochet is all in the wrists, so relax, and let's get started.

# Add It Up

A **foundation chain** has two sides. The side facing as you chain is called the top. And along the top, the stitches form a line of little "Vs". Each "V" has two strands: the strand that's nearest you (the right) is called the front loop, the strand farthest from you (the left) is called the back loop. The **new stitches** you form will be worked into these loops.

The side opposite the top is called the bottom (no surprise there, right?). On the bottom, the chain stitches form a single line of bumps. If you look at them closely you'll see that they are actually loops, too. They are called—yes, you guessed it—the bottom loops. Down the road you may encounter a few projects that call for crocheting into the **bottom loops**, but for now we'll stick to the top.

When you **count** crochet stitches (and you'll be doing this a lot) always count from the first stitch after the hook to the last stitch before the slip knot. In other words, the loop that's on the hook is **not** counted as a chain stitch, nor is the slip knot. We'll make it a bit clearer with the illustration far right.

## tip

Since there isn't a lot to hold on to, the first row of any crochet stitch is always the hardest to complete. Relax, take it slow and remember that things will get easier as you move on.

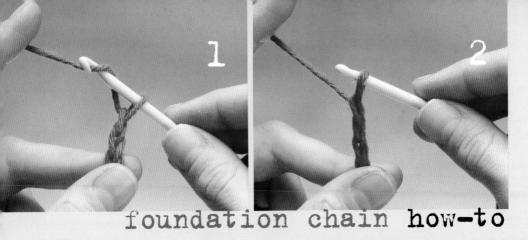

## foundation chain how-to

**1.** Lay the long end of the yarn over the hook from back to front.

**2.** Catch the yarn under the hook and draw the yarn through the loop.

In these next few chapters, we'll be teaching you a few **basic** stitches, with each stitch getting progressively taller. This is important because which chain stitch you dip into to make your first crochet stitch will determine the height of the finished stitch. So since one chain stitch equals the height of a **single** crochet stitch (which we'll cover in a minute), you'll make your first stitch into the second chain stitch from the hook. For a **half-double** crochet stitch you'll need two chain stitches to equal the height, so you will dip your hook into the third stitch from the hook. Confused? Don't worry. The pattern directions will always tell you where to begin.

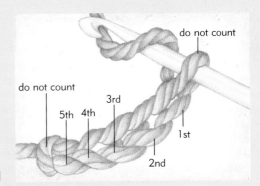

do not count

do not count

5th 4th 3rd

1st

2nd

# Single Crochet

Now that you've got the foundation down, you're ready to start stitching. We are going to show you that most basic of crochet stitches, the **single crochet**.

Start by making a foundation chain of 11 stitches, holding the **foundation chain** so that the top is facing you and your thumb and middle finger are holding the third stitch from the hook. Now follow the pictures above and instructions below and we'll get going.

## tip

Remember that one chain stitch equals the height of the single crochet stitch and that you will always turn the piece from right to left.

## single crochet how-to

1. Insert the hook under both the front and back loops of the second chain from the hook. Wrap the yarn over the hook from back to front (this is called a yarn over) and catch it on the hook. Now draw the hook through the two chain stitch loops. Like magic, you will now have two loops on the hook.

2. Wrap the yarn over the hook from the back to the front (yarn over), then draw the yarn over through both loops on the hook.

3. You have now completed one single crochet stitch. (That wasn't so hard, was it?) Now repeat steps 1 and 2 nine more times, inserting the hook into each chain stitch across. You'll now have ten single crochet stitches completed across the row.

# Chain It Up

It's time to **move** on to the next row. Make one chain stitch (this is called the turning chain), then turn the piece from the right to the left. In crochet lingo this is called **"chain and turn."** For the next row, insert the hook under both the front and back loops of the first stitch (skipping the one turning stitch). Repeat these steps until you have **completed** 10 rows of single crochet.

# here's how

When you've completed the **number** of rows or achieved the **length** called for in your pattern instructions, you'll need to secure the last stitch so that all your hard work doesn't unravel. This is called **fastening off,** and it's very easy to do.

# The End

So now that you know how to both start a stitch and finish it off, we're going to give you a few easy projects to try. Before you dive in, you should make yourself a **gauge swatch**, which is kind of a test run of how your pattern, yarn, hook and stitching style all work together. The details are the same as those given in the **knit section** (see page 23); it's just that you'll be looking at **crochet stitches** instead of knit stitches. You should also familiarize yourself with how to read instructions, the

# fastening off how-to

1. Start by cutting the yarn about 12 inches from the last loop on the hook. Bring the remaining yarn over the hook.

2. Draw the tail all the way through the loop on the hook.

Pull the tail to tighten, and voilá! Your stitches are safe and secure.

abbreviations used in crochet patterns (you'll see the whole shebang on pages 198–199), and how to choose the right size, measure your body, read a schematic and other goodies. You'll find that info in **Chapter 9** of the knit section, and it all applies just the same to crochet.

Now with that out of the way, let's get going on some **real stitching**....

So you want to be a rock star? Well, at least you'll look the part. Simple crochet is all you need to make this cool, practical guitar strap with matching wristbands.

## materials

**Straps**

1 ball in #140 Deep Rose of Wool-Ease® Chunky by Lion Brand, 5oz/140g ball, approx 153yd/140m (acrylic/wool)

2 balls in #194 Lime of Fun Fur by Lion Brand, 1¾oz/50g balls, each approx 60yd/45m (polyester)

**Wristbands**

1 ball in #194 Lime

Size J/10 (6.5mm) crochet hook OR SIZE TO OBTAIN GAUGE

## the measurements

Strap (slightly stretched) measures 58"/147cm long by 3"/7.5cm wide

Wristbands are 2"/5cm wide and desired length.

## the gauge

8 sc to 3"/7.5cm and 10 rows to 4"/10cm over sc pat st using 1 strand each Wool-Ease® Chunky and Fun Fur held tog and J/10 (6.5mm) hook.

BE SURE TO GET THE GAUGE.

## make the strap

■ With 1 strand each Fun Fur and Wool-Ease® Chunky held tog, ch 9.

■ **Row 1** Work 1 sc in 2nd ch from hook and 1 in each ch to end—8sc. Ch 1, turn on this and all foll rows. **Row 2** Work sc in each sc. Rep last row. Fasten off Wool-Ease® Chunky only.

## make the tassels

■ Cont to work with Fun Fur only, ch 11. Work sc in 2nd ch from hook, then sc in each ch to point of guitar strap.

■ Attach Fun Fur and work tassel on opposite end.

■ Attach one end of strap to the button nearest the guitar neck, pushing the button between the sts. Attach the other end to button on end of guitar, or, tie the strap to the guitar using Wool-Ease Chunky near the tuning pegs.

## make the wristbands

■ With 2 strands Fun Fur held tog, ch 9.

■ **Row 1** Work 1 sc in 2nd ch from hook and in each ch to end. Ch 1, turn on this and all foll rows. Rep row 1 until piece measures approx 6½"/16.5cm or desired length to fit wrist.

■ Sl st the short rnds tog to form the band.

# here's how

You can **single crochet** your way through any number of fabulous projects, but let's push the envelope a little, shall we? Now don't get all panicky on us; what we introduce in this chapter takes a little more **skill** and **concentration** than the old single crochet, but the stitches are still considered pretty **basic**. You will be able to do them. Honest....

Remember how we told you crochet stitches build on each other in height? Well we are going to put that theory into practice with a few new stitches. First up is the **half double crochet**, which starts with a foundation of twelve stitches. Got that done? Good. Now let's move on:

# Make Mine a Half Double

1. To begin a half double crochet stitch, yarn over.

2. Insert hook under the top 2 loops of the next stitch and yarn over.

3. Draw yarn-over through stitch; yarn over again.

4. Draw yarn-over through all 3 loops on the hook.

## half double crochet how to

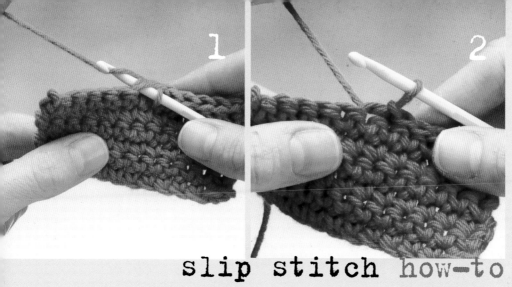

## slip stitch how-to

1. Insert the hook under both loops of the second chain from the hook. Yarn over the hook.

2. Draw through the chain stitch, then loop on the hook in one movement. You've made one slip stitch (yeah!).

# Slip Shape

Ready for one more? Let us introduce the slip stitch, a crochet oddity that's more about function than form. You'll use it to anchor chain stitches, shape pieces, make cording, join stitches when working in the round, secure seams, finish edges and a whole lot more. Every once in a while, you'll see it used in pattern stitches, but it's never worked on its own in multiple rows. Start by making a foundation chain of 11 stitches, then follow the simple steps above.

The **double crochet** stitch adds one more step to those you've completed in the half double crochet (which, by the way, is how the half double got its name). Start by making a foundation chain of 13 stitches, then follow the pretty pictures above and below:

# Twice as

## tip

It's easy to lose track of how many chain stitches you've made and how many are still left to make. To keep things straight, make yourself a cheat sheet. Write down the number of stitches you have to make on a sheet of paper. Each time you complete ten stitches, make a check mark on the paper. Continue until you reach the number of stitches called for in the pattern—so if you need 60 stitches, you'll have six check marks on your cheat sheet. Get it?

# double crochet how-to

1. To begin a double crochet stitch, yarn over.

2. Insert hook under the 2 top loops of the next stitch and yarn over again.

3. Draw the yarn-over through the stitch—3 loops are on hook; yarn over again.

4. Draw yarn-over through first 2 loops; yarn over.

5. Draw yarn-over through last 2 loops on hook.

# Nice: Double Crochet

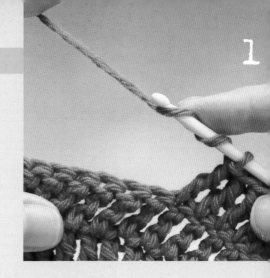

The next stitch we'd like you to meet is the **treble crochet**. This one builds on the double crochet stitch you learned earlier (beginning to see a pattern here?). To begin your first row, make a foundation chain of 14 stitches, then follow these easy (really!) steps.

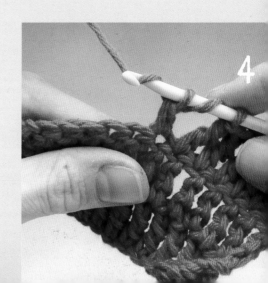

## treble crochet how-to

1. To begin a treble crochet stitch, yarn over twice.

2. Insert hook under the 2 top loops of the next stitch and yarn over once again.

3. Draw yarn-over through the stitch; yarn over once again.

4. Draw yarn-over through first 2 loops on hook; yarn over once again.

5. Draw yarn-over through next 2 loops, yarn over.

6. Draw yarn-over through last 2 loops on hook.

# We're in Treble

These scarves give your imagination free rein. Done primarily in double crochet, the look changes as easily as changing the yarn or adding fringe—your call.

## materials

**A:** 1 ball in #150 Silver of Glitterspun by Lion Brand, 1¾oz/50g ball, approx 115yd/105m (acrylic/polyester/cupro)

Size H/8 (5mm) crochet hook OR SIZE TO OBTAIN GAUGE OR

**B:** 1 ball in #204 Accent on Black of Incredible by Lion Brand, 1¾oz/50g ball, approx 110yd/100m (nylon)

Size K/10½ (6.5mm) crochet hook OR SIZE TO OBTAIN GAUGE OR

**C:** 1 ball in # 301 Night Life of Trellis by Lion Brand, 1¾oz/50g ball, approx 115yd/105m (nylon)

Size N/15 (10mm) crochet hook OR SIZE TO OBTAIN GAUGE

## the measurements

3"/7.5cm wide by 48"/122cm long without fringe

## the gauge

**A:** 14 sts to 3"/7.5cm and 7 rows to 4"/10cm in filet pat using Glitterspun and size H/8 (5mm) crochet hook.

**B:** 10 sts to 3"/7.5cm and 6 rows to 4"/10cm in filet pat using Incredible and size K/10½ (6.5mm) crochet hook.

**C:** 8 sts to 3"/7.5cm and 5 rows to 4"/10cm in filet pat using Trellis and size N/15 (10mm) crochet hook. BE SURE TO GET THE GAUGE.

## make the scarf

### A: GLITTERSPUN

■ Ch 18.

■ **Row 1** Work 1 dc in 6th ch from hook, [ch 1, skip next ch, 1 dc in next ch] 6 times, ch 4, turn. **Row 2** Skip first dc and work 1 dc in next dc, * ch 1, 1 dc in next dc; rep from * end last dc in 3rd ch of ch-4. Ch 4, turn. **Rows 3–84** Rep row 2. Fasten off at end of row 84.

## make the fringe

■ Cut 28 12-inch/30.5cm lengths of yarn. Fringe 2 lengths through each filet space at each end.

### B: INCREDIBLE

■ Ch 14.

■ **Row 1** Work 1 dc in 6th ch from hook, [ch 1, skip next ch, 1 dc in next ch] 4 times, ch 4, turn. **Row 2** Skip first dc and work 1 dc in next dc, * ch 1, 1 dc in next dc; rep from *, end last dc in 3rd ch of ch-4. Ch 4, turn. **Rows 3–72** Rep row 2. At end of row 72, fasten off.

## make the fringe

■ Cut 20 12-inch/30.5cm lengths of yarn. Fringe 2 lengths through each filet space at each end.

### C: TRELLIS

■ Ch 12.

■ **Row 1** Work 1 dc in 6th ch from hook, [ch 1, skip next ch, 1 dc in next ch] 3 times, ch 4, turn. **Row 2** Skip first dc and work 1 dc in next dc, * ch 1, 1 dc in next dc; rep from *, end last dc in 3rd ch of ch-4. Ch 4, turn. **Rows 3–60** Rep row 2. At end of row 60, fasten off.

## make the fringe

■ Cut 16 12-inch/30.5cm lengths of yarn. Fringe 2 lengths through each filet space at each end.

This appealing top is a great example of the versatility of crochet; it works equally well for shaping and embellishment. This tankini is sure to turn heads.

## materials

3 (4) balls in #143 Lavender; 1 ball each in #100 Lily White, #146 Fuchsia, #158 Buttercup, and #194 Lime, and small amount in #150 Sterling all of Microspun by Lion Brand, 2½oz/70g balls, each approx 168yd/154m (microfiber acrylic)

One each sizes E/4 and D/3 (3.5 and 3.25mm) crochet hooks OR SIZE NEEDED TO OBTAIN GAUGE

2 pair hook and eyes

Yarn needle

Sized for Small (Medium). Shown in size Small.

## the measurements

**Top**

Bust 27 (29)"/68.5 (73.5)cm (lacing at the back extends the bust measurement).
Length 8½ (9)"/21 (23)cm at center front

## the gauge

22 dc and 12 rows to 4"/10 cm in sc using size E/4 (3.5mm) hook.
BE SURE TO GET THE GAUGE.

**Notes** 1. Top is worked from above bust toward the waist. You then turn the piece upside down and work toward the neck along the foundation ch edge. 2. To work 2 dc tog: (Yo, insert hook in specified st, yo and draw up a loop, yo and draw through first 2 lps on hook) twice, yo and draw through 3 lps on hook—1 dec made.

## make the top

■ With Lavender, ch 152 (162). **Row 1 (RS)** Starting in third ch from hook, work dc in each ch across—150 (160) dc. Ch 2 (counts as first dc of next row), turn. **Row 2** Skip first dc, dc in each dc across. Ch 2, turn. **Row 3 (dec row)** Skip first dc, work 2 dc tog over next 2 dc, dc in each dc across to last 2 dc, 2 dc tog over last 2 dc—148 (158) dc. Ch 2, turn. **Rows 4–5, 7–8, 10–11, 13–17** Rep row 2. **Rows 6, 9 and 12** Rep row 3—142 (152) dc after row 12 has been completed.

■ For medium size only Work even in dc for 2 more rows.

■ For both sizes Fasten off. Turn piece to work along foundation ch edge. **Row 1** With RS facing, join lavender with sl st in first st, ch 1, sc in each of first 50 (53) sts, dc in

each of next 50 (54) sts, sc in each of last 50 sts (53) sts. Ch 1, turn. **Row 2** Sc in each of first 45 (48) sts, dc in each of next 60 (64) sts, sc in each of last 45 (48) sts. Ch 1, turn. **Row 3** Sc in each of first 40 (43) sts, dc in each of next 70 (74) sts, sc in each of last 40 (43) sts. Ch 1, turn. **Row 4** Sc in each of first 30 (32) sts, dc in each of next 90 (96) sts, sc in each of last 30 (32) sts. Ch 1, turn. **Row 5** Sc in each of first 20 (22) sts, dc in each of next 110 (116) sts, sc in each of last 20 (22) sts. Ch 1, turn. **Row 6** Sc in each of first 10 (11) sts, dc in each of next 130 (138) sts, sc in each of last 10 (11) sts. Ch 1, turn.

## make the flowers

**Note** Work with size D/3 (3.25mm) hook

■ **Flower 1** With Fuchsia, ch 5, join with sl st to first ch to form ring. **Rnd 1** Work [2 sc in ring, ch 3] 5 times. Join with sl st to first st. **Rnd 2** In each ch-3 sp work (1 sc, 1 hdc, 1 dc, 1 hdc, 1 sc). Join and fasten off.

■ **Flower 2** With Buttercup, ch 5, join with sl st to first ch to form ring. **Rnd 1** Work 10 sc in ring. Rnd 2 [Ch 8, skip 1 sc, sc in next sc] 5 times. **Rnd 3** In each ch-8 loop work 10 sc. Fasten off. **Rnd 4** With new color, join yarn in one skipped sc from rnd 2, *ch 3, sl st in next skipped sc from rnd 2; rep from * around–5 ch-3 loops. **Rnd 5** In each ch-3 loop work (1 sc, 1 hdc, 1 dc, 1 hdc, 1 sc). Join and fasten off.

■ **Flower 3** With White, ch 5, join with sl st to first ch to form ring. **Rnd 1** Work 10 sc in ring. **Rnd 2** [Ch 8, dc in 3rd ch from hook and in next 5 ch, sk next sc, sl st in next sc] 5 times. Fasten off. **Rnd 3** With 3 strands only of a new color, join yarn in one skipped sc from rnd 2, *ch 3, sl st in next skipped sc from rnd 2; rep from * around–5 ch-3 loops. Fasten off.

■ **Half-Leaf** With Lime, ch 8, sc in 2rd ch from hook, dc in each of next 6 ch. Fasten off,

■ **Full Leaf** With Lime, ch 8, sc in 2nd ch from hook, dc in each of next 5 ch, sc in last ch, work along foundation ch as foll: sc in next ch, dc in each of next 5 ch, sc in next ch. Fasten off.

## finish the top

■ Sew flowers in place on top as shown in photograph. With Lime, make a chain about 8"/20.5cm and sew it in place, curling it in a couple of places. With Silver Grey, work bullion sts around the flowers (see how-to opposite).

■ With RS of work facing, join Lavender in corner of top piece and work in sc around, working 3 sc at each corner, 150 (160) sc along the top edge, 142 (152) sc along the bottom edge and 38 (42) sc evenly spaced along each side edge.

■ With Lavender, make a 60"/153cm chain. Fasten off. Place 5 markers along each side edge of piece, 1 at top and bottom corners and 3 more evenly spaced between. Weave chain, shoelace fashion, between the side edges, having the ends at the top. Sew 1 pair of hook and eye at each of top and bottom corners.

■ To make a tassel, cut ten 5"/12.5cm lengths of lavender. Tie 8 strands tog in the middle with the 1 strand. Fold all strands in half together and tie the remaining strand around all yarn ends about ½"/1.3cm down from fold. Wrap the ends of the tie around the tassel and weave in the ends. Use the tie at the fold to tie the tassel at one end of the chain. Make another tassel in the same manner for the other end of the chain.

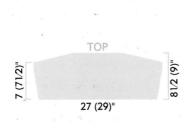

TOP

7 (7½)"

8½ (9)"

27 (29)"

11 (12)"

19 (21)"

9 (10)"

BOTTOM

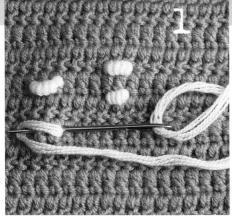

# bullion stitch

1. To make a bullion stitch, insert the yarn needle into fabric from front to back to front, and wrap yarn around needle. Wrap the yarn at least 7 or 8 times around the tip of the needle.

2. Pull the needle through all the wraps and secure.

# chain stitch

1. To make a chain stitch, insert hook into a stitch.

2. Wrap yarn around hook and pull it through the stitch and the loop on the hook.

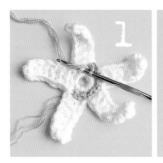

1. To make the center of the flower, split the strands to use three strands. Into skipped stitch from round 2, work a slip stitch and chain 3.

2. To complete a full leaf, work double crochet into each chain along the foundation chain.

# here's how

Sticking to the straight and narrow is just fine and dandy—if you want to crochet nothing more than skinny scarves and belts. (And hey, if you do, we're just fine with it.) But should you want to branch out into something a little more shapely—say, a sweater—you'll need to learn to **add** and **subtract stitches**, commonly known in the crochet world as **increasing** and **decreasing**.

# Gain Some—The Increase

Let's start with the increase. There are several ways to add stitches to your row; which method you use depends on where the stitch is being added.

1. Make the number of chain stitches you need to increase, then chain for the height of the stitch you are working in. Here, three stitches are going to be increased at the beginning of a single crochet row, so chain three for the increase and chain one for the height of the single crochet stitch—four chain stitches in total.

2. Work one single crochet in the 2nd chain from the hook, then work one single crochet in each of the next two chain stitches—three single crochet stitches made. Continue to work across the rest of the row.

## at the beginning of a row

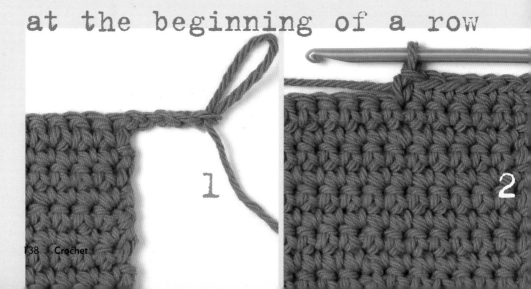

1

2

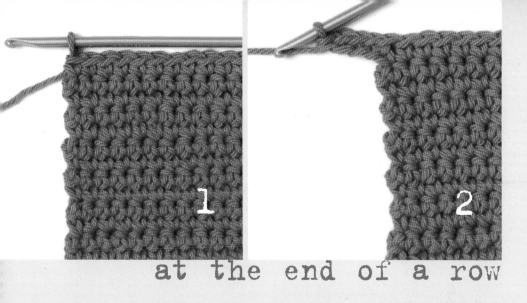

1.  To make the first increase stitch, insert the hook under the left vertical strand of the last single crochet stitch. Yarn over and draw up a loop. Yarn over and draw through both loops on the hook to complete the new single crochet stitch.

2. To make the next and all following increase stitches, insert the hook under the left vertical strand of the last single crochet stitch made. Yarn over and draw up a loop. Yarn over and draw through both loops on the hook to complete the new single crochet stitch.

## Increasing in the row

Really this is nothing more than working two or more stitches into one stitch. Confused?

Don't be. Simply work two stitches into the first stitch and two stitches into the last stitch.

## Increasing at the beginning of a row (see left)

You'll use this method when you need to add a stitch or two at the start of a row.

## Increasing at the end of row (see above)

Use this increase when you need to increase two or more stitches at the end of a row.

Here the example is worked in single crochet, but you can do it in any basic stitch.

Ups and Downs: Increasing and Decreasing

Now, let's move on to the decrease. As with the increase, you can do this several ways, each dependent on where the stitches need to be reduced.

## Decreasing in the row

The idea here is to work each stitch to within the last step to complete it, leaving the last loop (or loops) on the hook. You then yarn over and draw through all the loops on the hook to combine two (or more) stitches into one. Got it? No? Then let's go through it step by step:

# Lose Some—The Decrease

## Decreasing one single crochet

**1.** Insert the hook into the next stitch and draw up a loop. Insert the hook into the following stitch and draw up a loop.

**2.** Yarn over and draw through all three loops on the hook. One single crochet stitch is decreased.

## decreasing single crochet

# decreasing half double crochet

## Decreasing one half double crochet

1. Yarn over. Insert the hook into the next stitch and draw up a loop. Yarn over, insert the hook into the following stitch, and draw up a loop.

2. Yarn over and draw through all five loops on the hook. One half double crochet stitch is decreased.

## decreasing double crochet

### Decreasing one double crochet

1. Work 2 double crochet stitches together: [Yarn over. Insert the hook into the next stitch and draw up a loop. Yarn over and draw through two loops on the hook] twice.

2. Draw yarn-over through all three loops on the hook. One double crochet stitch has been decreased.

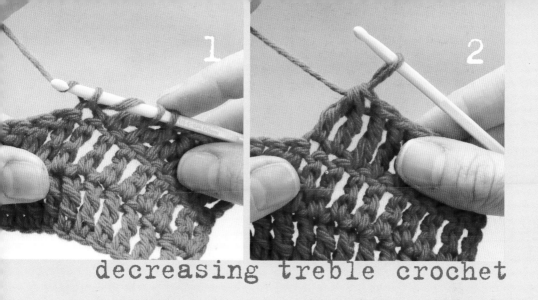

# decreasing treble crochet

## Decreasing one treble crochet

1. *Yarn over the hook twice. Insert the hook into the next stitch and draw up a loop. Yarn over, draw through two loops on the hook, then yarn over again and draw through two loops on the hook*.

Repeat from * to * in the following stitch.

2. Yarn over and draw through all three loops on the hook. One treble crochet stitch has been decreased.

## Decreasing at the beginning of a row

If you need to eliminate stitches at the beginning or end of a row, do it like this: Complete the last row before the decrease, then just turn the work (don't chain!). Work one slip stitch (remember those?) in each stitch that is to be decreased. Then chain for the height of the stitch you are working in (one for single, two for half double, etc.) and continue to work across the row.

## Decreasing at the end of a row

If your stitches need to be eliminated at the end of a row, work across the row to the last number of stitches to be decreased and leave them unworked. Chain and turn to work the next row.

Okay, now that you have the hang of sizing your rows up and down, let's move on to some projects with a little more shape to them....

For the furry friend in your life, here is a toy that's sure to please. Using the most basic crochet skills—a foundation chain and diminishing number of single crochets—it will be done in no time.

## materials

1 ball in #204 Bright Spring of Magic Stripes by Lion Brand, 3½oz/100g ball, approx 330yd/300m (wool/nylon)

Size D/3 (3.25mm) crochet hook OR SIZE TO OBTAIN GAUGE

Small amount of polyester fiberfill

Catnip (optional)

## finished measurements

Approx 5½"/14cm wide and 6"/15cm long

## the gauge

24 sts and 24 rows to 4"/10cm over sc using size D/3 (3.25mm) crochet hook.

BE SURE TO GET THE GAUGE.

## stitch glossary

sc3tog [Insert hook in next st, yo and draw up a loop] 3 times, yo and draw through all 4 loops on hook.

## make the fish

Make 3 triangles. Ch 34. **Row 1** Sc in 2nd ch from hook and in each ch across—33 sts. Ch 1, turn. **Row 2** Skip first st, sc in each st to last 2 sts, skip next st, sc in last st—31 sts. Ch 1, turn. **Rows 3–16** Rep row 2—3 sts. **Row 17** Sc3tog. Fasten off, leaving a long tail for sewing.

## finish the fish

Measure and mark center 1"/2.5cm along row 1 of 2 triangles. For the body and upper and lower fins, sew one side edge of these 2 triangles tog from row 17 to row 10, then using small running stitches, stitch an oval body outline ending at 1"/2.5cm opening. Rep for opposite edge and body outline. Stuff with fiberfill and optional catnip. Referring to photo, fold rem triangle in half for tail fin, then insert top edge into opening. Working through all layers, sew opening closed, securing tail fin in place.

swishy fish crocheted cat toy

Adorned with tassels and ties, this crocheted bikini is sure to turn heads at the beach. Show off your crochet shaping skills while showing off your shape.

## materials

2 balls in #100 Lily White of Microspun by Lion Brand, 2½oz/70g balls, each approx 168yd/154m (microfiber acrylic)

Size D/3 (3mm) crochet hook OR SIZE TO OBTAIN GAUGE

Sized for one size, size Small

## the measurements

Hip (tied as shown and adjustable) 32"/81.5cm

Bust cup 6½"/16.5cm across

## the gauge

17 dc and 10 rows to 4"/10cm over dc pat st using size D/3 (3mm) hook. BE SURE TO GET THE GAUGE.

## make the bottom

■ Beg at top back edge, ch 53. **Row 1** Starting in 4th ch from hook, dc in each ch across—51 dc, counting turning ch as 1 dc. Ch 3, turn, **Row 2** Skip first dc, (yo and draw up a lp in next st, yo and draw through all 2 lps on hook) twice, yo and draw through all 3 lps for dec 1 dc, dc in each dc to last 2 dc, dec 1 dc—49 dc. Ch 3, turn. **Rows 3–23** Work as for row 2—7 dc rem after row 23 is completed. **Rows 24–27** Work even in dc. Row 28 Dc in first dc, sc in each dc across to last dc, 2 dc in last dc—9 dc. Ch 3, turn. **Row 29** Work as for row 28—11 dc. **Rows 31–43** Work as for row 28—37 dc after row 43 is completed. Do not fasten off.

## make the edge

■ Cont along the side edge of piece and working to cover the last st of each row, work sc evenly along side edge, 3 sc in corner, sc evenly along top of front edge, 3 sc in corner, sc evenly along side edge, 3 sc in corner, sc evenly along top of back edge, then cont around, work 1 sc in each sc, (sc, ch 1, sc) in each corner along the side, front and side. Join and fasten off.

crocheted bikini

## make four ties

■ Join in ch-1 sc at corner, ch for 14"/36cm. Fasten off. Trim tie with a 3"/7.5cm tassel. Rep for each of 3 rem corners.

## make the top

(Make 2 identical pieces. The 2nd piece will be turned to the opposite side for mirror image shaping.)

■ Ch 27. **Row 1** Starting in 4th ch from hook, dc in each ch across—25 dc, including turning ch, Ch 3 (counts as 1 dc), turn. **Row 2** Skip first dc, dc in each dc across. Ch 3, turn. **Row 3** Dc in first st, dc across to last st, 2 dc in last st—27 dc. Ch 1, turn. **Row 4** Sc in each of first 7 dc, hdc in next dc, dc in each dc across. Ch 3, turn. **Row 5** Work as for row 2. Ch 3, turn. Row 6 Work as for row 3—29 dc. Ch 1, turn. **Row 7** Sc in each of first 13 dc, 2 hdc in next dc, dc in each dc across—30 sts. Ch 1, turn. **Row 8** sc in each of first 8 sts, hdc in next st, dc in each of next 7 sts—16 sts. Ch 3, turn. **Row 9** Work as for row 2—16 dc. Ch 3, turn. **Row 10** Skip first dc, dc in each of next 2 dc, dec 1 dc, dc in each dc across—15 dc. Ch 3, turn.

Row 11 Work as for row 2. Ch 1, turn. **Row 12** Sc in each of first 7 sts, hdc in next st, dc in each rem st. Ch 3, turn. **Row 13** Skip first dc, dc in each of next 2 sts, dec 1 dc, dc in each rem st—14 dc. Ch 3, turn. Row 14 Work as for row 2. Fasten off. Sew the edge of last 7 rows worked to the 14 free sts on row 8.

## make the trim

■ Work in sc evenly around each cup. Place the 2 cups on a flat surface so that row 1 of one cup is at outer right and row 1 of other cup is at outer left. Mark the joined edge on each piece for bottom edge and side of cup facing you as the right side. **Rnd 1 (RS)** Join yarn in lower right corner of one cup and work 1 rnd sc evenly spaced around outer edge of cup, working 3 sc in each corner, join. Ch 5 (counts as 1 dc, ch 2), turn to WS to work along bottom edge. **Rnd 2** Skip next sc, *dc in next sc, ch 2, skip next sc; rep from * across, sc in last sc on bottom edge; turn piece to RS and work reverse sc (from left to right) around next 2 sides of cup (not along bottom edge). Fasten off. Trim rem cup in same way.

## make the ties

■ Join yarn at top point of each cup and ch for 24"/60cm for neck ties. Ch a 82"/208cm tie and weave it through the drawstring row at the lower edge of each cup. Make 4 tassels as for bottom and tie one to end of each tie.

It's a wrap! This kerchief works up quickly
with a big hook and thick yarn. Finish off with fringe
and hit the town.

## materials

3 balls in #275 Autumn Trails of Landscapes by Lion Brand, 1¾ oz/50g balls, each approx 55yds/50m
(50% acrylic, 50% wool)
One size K-10½ (6.5mm) crochet hook, OR SIZE TO OBTAIN GAUGE

## the measurements

Width along top long edge 26"/66cm

Depth from top edge to bottom point 15½"/39cm

## the gauge

9 sts and 4 rows to 4"/10cm with K-10½ hook. BE SURE TO GET THE GAUGE.

**Notes** 1 Turning ch-2 does not count as a st. 2 Do not work last st of row into turning ch. 3 Work through
front loop only of each st.

## make the kerchief

■ Beg at bottom point, ch 2. **Row 1 (WS)** Work 2 dc in first ch. Ch 2, turn. **Row 2** Work 1 dc in first dc,
2 dc in next dc—3 dc. Ch 2, turn. **Row 3** Work 1 dc in each dc to last dc, 4 dc in last dc—3 dc inc
made—6 dc total. Ch 2, turn. **Rows 4–18** Work as for row 3—51 dc at end of row 18. Fasten off.

## make the fringe

■ Cut 2"/5cm lengths for each fringe. Knot 2 strands in end of each row and in bottom point. Knot the
fringe with knot showing on RS.

Up to this point we've been playing it straight, stitching along in nice even rows. Now, let's take crocheting in the round for a **spin**. To do this you can work in a **spiral** or **join rounds**. Once you master these two techniques you pave the way for a whole new world of crochet possibilities: hats, booties, bags, not to mention the ever-popular granny square. **Rounds** can shape up into a single item (a hat, for instance) or you can connect several smaller ones to create a kind of circular patchwork piece. You can also use them to make fab **flowers**, **medallions** and lots of other lovelies.

# Make a Ring

No matter what you are making or which method you're using, all rounds start with a **ring**. Whether that ring is a tightly closed circle (the crown of a hat, for example), or an open tube (say a sleeve cuff) depends on the number of chain stitches you start with. We'll demonstrate with a tight start:

1. To make a practice ring, chain six. Insert the hook through both loops of the first chain stitch made. Yarn over and draw through the chain stitch and the loop on the hook in one movement.

2. You have now joined the chain with a slip stitch and formed a ring.

# ring how-to

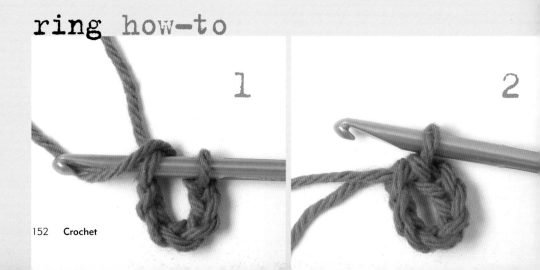

## spiral how-to

1. Chain five. Join the chain with a slip stitch, forming a ring. Work ten single crochets in the ring. Fasten a safety pin in the last stitch made to indicate the end of a round.

2. Work two single crochets in each of the first nine stitches. Unfasten the safety pin from the last stitch. Work two single crochets in the last stitch. Refasten the safety pin in the last stitch made—you now have twenty stitches. To practice one more round, * work one single crochet in the next stitch, then work two single crochets in the following stitch. Repeat from the * to the end of the round, unfastening, then refastening the safety pin in the last stitch —you now have thirty stitches.

# Spiraling

Spirals are worked around and around without **interruption**, usually in single or half double crochet (so there won't be a big difference in height at the beginning and end of the round).

## tip

While you are spiraling, it can be tricky to keep track of increases from one round to the next. Use a split-ring marker or small safety pin to mark the end of each round and keep count on a pad of paper as you go.

# here's how

**Joined rounds** can be used for any height of stitch because the beginning and end of each round are always of equal height. Essentially a series of concentric circles, all rounds begin with a chain stitch that equals the height of the stitch being used. A slip stitch in the first stitch joins the round and completes the circle. It's a little harder to work than a spiral, but since you can see where each round begin and ends, it's also easier to keep track of your increases.

## Working joined rounds

You can change yarns and colors within rounds to create some pretty striking pieces to be used on their own or stitched together to make a larger piece of fabric. Here's how to create a fab flower (we'll show you how to join several of them into a hip handbag on page 168).

1. Chain five. Join the chain with a slip stitch, forming a ring. Chain three (equals the height of a double crochet stitch). Work twelve double crochets in the ring, then join the round with a slip stitch in the top two loops of the first stitch.

2. For the second round, chain three. Work two double crochet in each of the twelve stitches. Join the round with a slip stitch in the first stitch—you now have twenty-four stitches. To practice one more round, chain three, *work one double crochet in the next stitch, then work two double crochet in the following stitch. Repeat from the * to the end of the round. Join the round with a slip stitch in the first stitch—you now have thirty-six stitches.

# joined rounds how-to

# flower how-to

1. To begin all the flowers, chain 5. Insert crochet hook into first chain made, as shown above. Then yarn over the hook, pull up a loop and pull through the loop on the hook to make a ring. Instructions for all the flowers can be found in the patterns pages.

2. To make the first round of all of the flowers, chain 3, which counts as the first half-double crochet (hdc) and chain 1;

continue to work (1 hdc and chain 1) 11 times. You will have 12 hdc and 12 chain-1 spaces. Join the round by working a slip stitch into the 2nd chain of the beginning chain 3. This completes flower 1.

3. Shown here is round 3, or the last round of flower 2. By working (1 sc, 2 hdc and 1 sc) into each chain-1 space from the previous round, you create a ruffled edge. This completes flower 2.

Here's how to crochet some of the flowers used on the tank top and bag at the end of this chapter.

# Simple Steps to Make Your Projects Bloom

## tip

There are no set rules about increases, but generally speaking, the taller the stitch and the thinner the yarn, the more stitches you'll work in the first round and all rounds thereafter. Oh, and sometimes, there'll be no increases at all. Just go with it.

# Great Grannies

For good or bad, the **granny square** is the stitch most people visualize when you mention "crochet." We'll bet almost everyone you know has an **afghan** their grandma made using this nifty variation on the basic crochet round. And like most grannies, she can do a lot of things you never expected of her. Here's how it works:

1. With the first color, ch 4. Join ch with a sl st forming a ring. For round 1, ch 3 (counts as 1 dc), working in the ring, work two more dc for the first 3-dc group as shown, then ch 2 for the first corner ch-2 sp.

2. To complete the round, [work 3 dc in ring, ch 2] 3 times. (Note As you crochet around, work the dc groups over the tail of the ring or tail from the previous round so you won't have to weave them in later.) This gives you three more 3-dc groups and three more corner ch-2 sps. Join the rnd with a sl st in the top of the beg ch-3 (the first "dc"). Fasten off.

3. From the RS, join the next color in any corner ch-2 sp with a sl st. (Note Always alternate the corner you join the color in, so joins are evenly distributed.)

# granny square how-to

4. For round 2, ch 3 (counts as 1 dc), work 2 dc in same ch-2 sp (this forms the first half of the first corner), ch 1, [work (3 dc, ch 2, 3 dc) in next ch-2 sp, ch 1] 3 times, at the end work 3 dc in beg ch-2 sp, ch 2 (this forms the second half of the first corner). Join the rnd with a sl st in the top of the beg ch-3. Fasten off. You now have four ch-2 corner sps and four ch-1 sps (one on each side).

5. Join the next color with a sl st in any corner ch-2 sp. For round 3, ch 3, work 2 dc in same ch-2 sp, ch 1, [work 3 dc in next ch-1 sp, ch 1, work (3 dc, ch 2, 3 dc) in next ch-2 sp, ch 1] 3 times, end work 3 dc in next ch-1 sp, ch 1, work 3 dc in beg ch-2 sp, ch 2. Join rnd with a sl st in top of beg ch-3. Fasten off. You still have four ch-2 corner sps, but now you have eight ch-1 sps (two on each side). For every round that follows, you will increase one ch-1 sp on each side.

This poncho combines a simple mesh pattern stitch with dramatic, fringed embellishment. This is one garment you'll wear everywhere.

## materials

6 balls in #204 Accent on Black of Incredible by Lion Brand, 1¾oz/50g balls, each approx 110yd/100m (nylon)

One each sizes I/9 (5.5mm) and K/10½ (6.5mm) crochet hooks OR SIZE TO OBTAIN GAUGE

## finished measurements

One size to fit a 32–40"/81–102cm bust

**Width at lower edge** 66"/168cm

**Neck** 28"/71cm

**Length** (excluding fringe) 18"/45.5cm

## the gauge

11 sts and 6 rows/rnds to 4"/10cm over mesh pat st using larger hook. BE SURE TO GET THE GAUGE.

**Note** Each sc will count as 1 and each ch-1 space will count as 1 st for accurate stitch counts.

## mesh pattern stitch

▨ Chain an even number of sts, join with sl st to first ch to form ring. **Rnd 1** Ch 4 (counts as 1 dc and ch -1 space), *skip next ch, 1 dc in next ch, ch 1; rep from * to last ch, skip last ch and join with sl st to 3rd ch of ch-4. **Rnd 2** Sl st in first ch-1 space, ch 4 (counts as 1 dc and ch-1 space), skip next dc, *1 dc in next ch-1 space, ch 1, skip 1 dc; rep from * around, end join with sl st to 3rd ch of ch-4. Rep rnd 2 for mesh pat st.

## make the poncho

▨ Beg at lower edge and using larger hook, ch 184. Join with sl st to first ch to join ring, being careful not to twist the chain. Work rnd 1 of mesh pat st on 184 sts.

▨ Rep rnd 2 of mesh pat st until piece measures 7"/18cm from beg.

## shape the top

▨ **Rnd 1** Sl st in first ch-1 space, ch 4 (counts as 1 dc and ch-1 space), [skip next dc, 1 dc in next ch-1 space, ch 1] 20 times, skip next dc, *yo and draw up a loop in next ch-1 space, yo and draw through 2 loops on hook, skip next dc, yo and draw up a loop in next ch-1 space, yo and draw through 2 loops on hook, yo and draw through all loops on hook—2-st dec made, [ch 1, skip next dc, 1 dc in next ch-1 space] 21 times, ch 1, skip next dc; rep from * to last 4 sts, work 2-st dec, ch 1, join with sl st to 3rd ch of ch-4—176 sts.

**Rnd 2** Work even.

**Rnd 3** Sl st in first ch-1 space, ch 4, [skip next dc, 1 dc in next ch-1 space, ch 1] 19 times, skip next dc, *work 2-st dec, [ch 1, skip next dc, 1 dc in next ch-1 space] 20 times, ch 1, skip next dc; rep from * twice more, work 2-st dec, ch 1, join—168 sts.

**Rnds 4 and 6** Work even.

**Rnds 5 and 7** Work 2-st dec 4 times as before on each rnd—152 sts at end of rnd 7.

**Rnd 8** Work even.

**Rnd 9** Sl st in ch-1 space, ch 4, [skip next dc, 1 dc in ch-1 space, ch 1] 16 times, skip next dc, *work 2-st dec, [ch 1, skip next dc, 1 dc in ch-1 space] 17 times, ch 1, skip next dc; rep from * twice more, work 2-st dec, ch 1, join—144 sts.

**Rnd 10** Sl st in ch-1 space, ch 4, [skip next dc, 1 dc in ch-1 space, ch 1] 7 times, skip next dc, *work 2-st dec, [ch 1, skip next dc, 1 dc in ch-1 space] 16 times, ch 1, skip next dc; rep from * twice more, work 2-st dec, ch 1, [skip next dc, 1 dc in ch-1 space, ch 1] 8 times, join—136 sts.

**Rnd 11** Sl st in ch-1 space, ch 4, [skip next dc, 1 dc in ch-1 space, ch 1] 14 times, skip next dc, *work 2-st dec, [ch 1, skip next dc, 1 dc in ch-1 space] 15 times, ch 1, skip next dc; rep from * twice more, work 2-st dec, ch 1, join—128 sts.

**Rnd 12** Sl st in ch-1 space, ch 4, [skip next dc, 1 dc in ch-1 space, ch 1] 6 times, skip next dc, *work 2-st dec, [ch 1, skip next dc, 1 dc in ch-1 space] 14 times, ch 1, skip next dc; rep from * twice more, work 2-st dec, ch 1, [skip next dc, 1 dc in ch-1 space, ch 1] 7 times, ch1, join—120 sts.

**Rnd 13** Sl st in ch-1 space, ch 4, [skip next dc, 1 dc in ch-1 space, ch 1] 12 times, skip next dc, *work 2-st dec, [ch 1, skip next dc, 1 dc in ch-1 space] 13 times, ch 1, skip next dc; rep from * twice, work 2-st dec, ch 1, join—112 sts.

**Rnd 14** Sl st in ch-1 space, ch 4, [skip next dc, 1 dc in ch-1 space, ch 1] 4 times, skip next dc, *work 2-st dec, [ch 1, skip next dc, 1 dc in ch-1 space] 5 times, ch 1, skip next dc; rep from * 6 times more, work 2-st dec, ch 1, join—96 sts.

**Rnd 15** Sl st in ch-1 space, ch 4, [skip next dc, 1 dc in ch-1 space, ch 1] 3 times, skip next dc, *work 2-st dec, [ch 1, skip next dc, 1 dc in ch-1 space] 4 times, ch 1, skip next dc; rep from * 6 times more, work 2-st dec, ch 1, join—80 sts.

■ Change to smaller hook. Last rnd Sl st in ch-1 space, ch 1, 1 sc in same space with joining, 1 sc in each dc and in each ch-1 space around, join and fasten off.

## make the fringe

■ For each fringe, cut two 14"/36cm lengths of yarn.

■ Knot 2 strands each ch-1 space along lower edge of poncho.

This headband can be worn for a special occasion or just to feel special. Glittery yarn and attention to finished detail make this piece an everyday heirloom.

## materials

1 ball each in #150 Silver (MC) and #170 Gold (CC) of Glitterspun by Lion Brand, 1¾oz/50g balls, each approx 115 yd/105m (acrylic/cupro/polyester)

Size F/5 (3.75mm) crochet hook OR SIZE TO OBTAIN GAUGE

Silver or white fabric-covered headband

Three ⅜"/10mm crystal rhinestone buttons

Matching thread

Sewing needle

Thick designer craft glue

Toothpicks

## the gauge

Large rose is approx 3"/7.5cm wide using size F/5 (3.75mm) crochet hook. BE SURE TO GET THE GAUGE.

## make the large rose

With MC, ch 6.

**First row of petals. Rnd 1 (RS)** In the 6th ch from hook, work [dc and ch 2] 7 times, join rnd with a sl st in 3rd ch of ch-6—8 ch-2 sps. **Rnd 2** Ch 1, work (sc, ch 1, 2 dc, ch 1, sc) in each ch-2 sp around, join rnd with a sl st in first sc. Fasten off.

**Second row of petals.** With CC, make a slip knot and place on hook. With RS of flower facing, fold first row of petals towards you. Insert hook around any dc of rnd 1, making a sl st to join yarn. **Rnd 3** Ch 6 (counts as 1 dc and ch 3), *dc around next dc of rnd 1, ch 3; rep from * around 6 times more, join rnd with a sl st in 3rd ch of beg ch-6—8 ch-3 sps. **Rnd 4** Ch 1, work (sc, ch 1, 3 dc, ch 1, sc) in each ch-3 sp around, join rnd with a sl st in first sc. Fasten off.

**Third row of petals.** With MC, make a slip knot and place on hook. With RS of flower facing, fold first and second rows of petals towards you. Insert hook around any dc of rnd 3, making a sl st to join yarn. **Rnd 5** Ch 7 (counts as 1 dc and ch 4), *dc around next dc of rnd 3, ch 4; rep from * around 6 times more, join rnd with a sl st in 3rd ch of beg ch-7—8 ch-4 sps. **Rnd 6** Ch 1, work (sc, ch 1, 4 dc, ch 1, sc) in each ch-4 sp around, join rnd with a sl st in first sc. Fasten off.

## make small roses

For first rose, work as for large rose until second row of petals is completed.

For second rose, work first row of petals using CC and second row of petals using MC.

## finish the headband

Glue one end of MC to bottom WS tip of headband. Let dry, then wrap MC around headband in even concentric rows to opposite tip. Draw end to WS, then secure end with a dot of glue. Sew buttons to center of roses. Sew or glue roses to headband as shown.

The use of motifs could not be further from the traditional afghan granny square. The openness of the design, complemented by delicate ties, completes the elegant look. Fabric paint applied with a sponge lets you pick the perfect amount of color.

## materials

3 balls in #100 White of Lion Cotton by Lion Brand, 5oz/140g balls, each approx 236yds/215m (cotton)
Fabric paint and sponge
Two 1.5cm wooden beads with large center holes
One each size F-5 and G-6 (3.75 and 4mm) crochet hooks OR SIZE TO OBTAIN GAUGE

## finished measurements

Width along top long edge 49"/124.5cm
Depth from top edge to bottom point 24"/61cm

## the gauge

**Rnds 1 and 2** measure 2½"/6.5cm in diameter; completed motif measures 3½"/9cm in diameter with F-5 (3.75mm) hook. BE SURE TO GET THE GAUGE.

**Notes** 1. Start joining motifs to one another on rnd 3 of second motif. 2. To work cluster st: (Yo, insert hook and draw up a lp, yo and draw through 2 lps on hook) 3 times in same st, yo and draw through all 4 lps on hook.

## make the shawl

■ First Motif Ch 4, join with sl st to first ch to form a ring.

**Rnd 1** Ch 1, work 8 sc in ring, join with sl st to first sc.

**Rnd 2** Ch 3, [(yo, insert hook and draw up a lp, yo and draw through 2 lps on hook) twice in same first sc, yo and draw through all 3 lps on hook—starting cluster made], ch 4, (cluster in next sc, ch 4) 7 times, join with sl st to top of starting cluster.

**Rnd 3** Sl st in next ch-4 space, ch 1, *work (sc, ch 2, sc, ch 4, sc) in next ch-4 space, ch 8 (for corner), (sc, ch 4, sc, ch 2, sc) in next ch-4 space; rep from * around, join with sl st to first sc. Fasten off.

## join the motifs

■ Refer to chart to determine on how many sides a motif will be joined.

■ Join on Rnd 3 of motif, joining in corresponding ch-8 corners or ch-4 lps only.

■ To join 2 ch-8 corners, work ch 4 on rnd 3 of second motif, drop lp from hook, insert hook from front to back through corresponding ch-8 lp on first motif, pick up dropped lp of second motif, ch 4, cont to work rnd 3 on second motif as established.

■ To join 2 ch-4 lps, work ch 2 on rnd 3 of second motif, drop lp from hook, insert hook from front to back in corresponding ch-4 lp on first motif, pick up dropped lp of second motif, ch 2, continue to work rnd 3 of second motif as established.

■ Make a total of 49 motifs, joined in formation shown on placement diagram.

## make the edging

Work across top long edge of joined motifs: With right side of work facing, join yarn in first ch-4 sp to left of corner ch-8 sp of marked motif on placement diagram. *(Sc, ch 4, sc) in next ch-4 sp, sc in next ch-2 sp, ch 2, sc in next ch-2 sp, (sc, ch 4, sc) in next ch-4 sp**, (sc, ch 4, sc ) in next ch-8 lp, ch 1, (sc, ch 4, sc) in next ch-8 lp; rep from * across to last motif of long edge, work along last motif ending at **. Work across end of last motif on long edge: Work [(sc, ch 2) 3 times, sc] in next ch-8 lp, work (sc, ch 4, sc) in next ch-4 sp, dc in next ch-2 sp, tr in next sc, ch 3, sc in third ch from hook, tr in next sc, dc in next ch-2 sp, (sc, ch 4, sc) in next ch-4 sp. Work along left side edge of joined motifs: *Work [(sc, ch 2) 3 times, sc] in next ch-8 lp , work (sc, ch 4, sc) in next ch-4 sp, sc in next ch-2 sp, ch 2, sc in next ch-2 sp, (sc, ch 4, sc) in next ch-4 sp, dc in next ch-8 lp, dc in ch-8 lp on next motif, (sc, ch 2) in next ch-4 sp and mark this sp, drop lp, insert hook from front to back through last ch-4 sp made, pick up dropped lp, ch 4, work sc in last ch-2 sp made, ch 2, sc again in marked sp), sc in next ch-2 sp, ch 2, (sc, ch 4, sc) in next ch-4 space; repeat from * across to bottom single motif. Work across end of last motif in same manner as for last motif on long edge above. Work across right side edge of joined motifs as for left side edge above. Work across end of first motif in manner established. Work [(sc, ch 2) 3 times, sc] in next ch-8 lp, join with sl st to first sc. Fasten off.

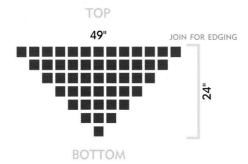

TOP

49"

JOIN FOR EDGING

24"

BOTTOM

## finish the shawl

■ Weave in and trim all ends on WS of work. Place shawl WS up on flat surface and block lightly.

■ Make ties. Cut one 3yd/2.75m length of yarn for each of 2 ties. Fold yarn in half and with larger hook draw up the center of the folded lp through the 6th ch-4 sp from one corner on top long edge, ch 40 with doubled strand. Fasten off, leaving a 6"/15cm end. Work remaining tie in same manner in 6th ch-4 sp from opposite corner.

■ Cut three 12"/30.5cm lengths of yarn for each tie tassel. Pull a bead over the end of each tie. Pull the tassel lengths through the last ch on each tie and make a knot with the yarn ends. Trim yarn ends.

■ If desired, dip sponge lightly in fabric paint and sponge over the surface of the right side of the shawl as shown in photograph.

## materials

2 balls each in #137 Fuchsia and #104 Blush Heather of Wool Ease® by Lion Brand, 3oz/85g ball, approx 197yd/180m (acrylic/wool)

1 ball in #177 Sage of Lion Suede by Lion Brand, 3oz/85g ball, approx 122yd/110m (acrylic)

1 ball each in #195 Hot Pink, #101 Soft Pink and #194 Lime of Fun Fur by Lion Brand, 1¾oz/50g balls, approx 60yd/54m (polyester)

1 ball in #170 Gold of Glitterspun by Lion Brand, 1¾oz/50g balls, each approx 115yd/105m (acrylic/cupro/polyester)

1 ball in #306 Pastel Garden of Trellis by Lion Brand, 1¾oz/50g ball, approx 115yd/105m (nylon)

Size G/6 (4mm) crochet hook OR SIZE TO OBTAIN GAUGE

Two metal clasps

¾yd/.68m of ⅝"/1.5cm-wide ribbon

2yd/1.8m of ⅜"/1cm braided cord

4"/10cm x 9"/23cm piece of cardboard

Two 14"/35.5cm x 7"/18cm pieces of lining material for sides and one 5"/12.5cm x 10"/25.5cm piece for base (optional)

4 metal feet for purse base

Sewing machine or sewing thread and needle

## the measurements

Approx 10"/25.5cm wide by 8"/20.5cm tall

## the gauge

7 mesh sts (1 mesh st = 2 dc plus ch 1) and 12 rows to 4"/10cm over mesh pat using size G/6 (4mm) crochet hook. BE SURE TO GET THE GAUGE.

## mesh pattern

**Rnd 1** *2 dc in next ch-1 sp, ch 1; rep from * around. Rep rnd 1 for mesh pat. As the rnds are not joined, carry a yarn marker while working to mark beg of rnds.

## make the base

With Fuchsia, ch 23. **Row 1** Sc in 2nd ch from hook and in each ch across—22 sc. Ch 1, turn. **Row 2** Sc in each sc. Ch 1, turn. Rep row 2 until there are a total of 48 rows from beg. Do not fasten off.

## make the bag

**Note** Ch 2 for first dc of next row.

**Foundation rnd** Turn to work along long edge of base, *work [2 dc in end of next row, ch 1, skip 2 rows] 16 times; working along short edge, [work 2 dc in next st; ch 1, skip 2 sts] 7 times, 2 dc in next sc, ch 1; rep from * once more—48 mesh. Work in mesh pat until piece measures 6"/15cm from beg. **Next rnd** Work sc in each dc and ch-1 sp around. Work even in sc for 4 more rnds. **Next rnd** Ch 2, dc in same sc, ch 1, skip 2 sc, *2 dc in next sc, ch 1, skip 2 sc; rep from *

Sure to become one of your favorites, this hip Flower Bag boasts a rare combination of style and functionality. It boasts lots of finishing detail, including metal clasps, ribbon trim and braided cord handles.

flower bag

around. Work 2 more rnds even in mesh pat. Work 1 rnd reverse sc (work as for sc, but work from left to right instead of right to left), join with sl st to first reverse sc. Fasten off.

## make the flowers

**Note** Use the foll color key when making flowers: A = Fuchsia; B = Blush Heather; C = Sage; D = Hot Pink; E = Soft Pink; F = Lime; G = Gold; H = Pastel Garden

## Basic flower

■ With Color 1 (see below), ch 5. Join with sl st to first ch to form ring. **Rnd 1** Ch 3 (counts as first hdc and ch 1), [1 hdc in ring, ch 1] 11 times, end sl st in top of 2nd ch of ch-3. **Rnd 2** Yo hook, insert hook from back to front to back around ch 2 from rnd 1, [yo and through 2 lps] twice for back post dc (bpdc), ch 2, *work bpdc around next hdc from rnd 1, ch 2; rep from * around, end sc in top of first st. Fasten off. **Rnd 3** Change to Color 2. In each ch-2 sp work 3 hdc–36 hdc in total. Fasten off. Extra rnd Change to Color 3. Working from RS, in each ch-1 sp from rnd 1, work (1 sc, 1 hdc and 1 sc).

■ Make 12 flowers in total. Work 1 in each of the foll color combinations: (Note When 2 yarns are given for 1 color, work with the two held tog as one):

■ **Flower 1** Color 1: B, Color 2: F + H, Color 3: A. Flower 2 Color 1: B, Color 2: E + H, Color 3: G. Flower 3 Color 1: B, Color 2: F + H, Color 3: G. Flower 4 Color 1: B, Color 2: D + H, Color 3: G. Flower 5 Color 1: A, Color 2: F + H, Color 3: B. Flower 6 Color 1: A, Color 2: D + H, Color 3: B. Flower 7 Color 1: A, Color 2: E + H, Color 3: B. Flower 8 Color 1: C, Color 2: E + H, Color 3: A. Flower 9 Color 1: C, Color 2: D + H, Color 3: B. Flower 10 Color 1: C, Color 2: E + H, Color 3: A. Flower 11 Color 1: G, Color 2: D + H, Color 3: C. Flower 12 Color 1: G, Color 2: F + H, Color 3: C.

## finish the bag

■ After all flowers have been made, sew 2 rows of 3 flowers each on front of bag; repeat on back of bag.

■ Cut 2 pieces of ribbon each 9½"/24cm long. Insert each end of one piece of ribbon through the base of a clasp; fold back a ½"/1.3cm loop to WS and sew clasps in place. Fold back ½"/1.3cm to WS at each end of remaining 9½"/24cm piece of ribbon; sew ends in place. Cut two 1½"/3.8cm-long pieces of ribbon; fold each piece in half width-wise and stitch along open edges; fold piece in half lengthwise to form a loop; pin loop to wrong side of each end of hemmed ribbon without clasps so that ½"/1.3cm extends; sew in place. Set ribbon pieces aside.

■ Cut braided cord in 4 equal pieces for handles. Set handles aside. Adhere cardboard to bottom of bag with fabric glue. Insert one metal foot at each corner of crocheted base and cardboard together; secure.

■ Lining Place 2 same-size pieces of lining material RS tog. Sew a ½"/1.3cm seam along each 7"/18 cm edge. Having each side seam at center of each short edge, pin base to bottom of bag and sew in place with a ½"/1.3cm seam. Turn down top ½"/1.3cm of lining bag to outside of bag and sew in place. Place lining in bag with top edge even with top row of sc; pin in place. Center and pin one finished ribbon to each side of bag at same level with lining. Mark the center 3"/7.5cm at top of each ribbon. Insert the ends of one handle piece under ribbon at each end of marked portion and pin in place; insert the ends of another handle piece at each side of previous ends and pin in place. Rep on opposite side of bag. Stitching through all layers, top-stitch around all four sides of ribbon, catching the ribbon, cords and lining at one time. Hook each clasp into corresponding ribbon loop on opposite side of bag.

1. To begin all the flowers, chain 5. Insert crochet hook into first chain made, as shown above. Then yarn over the hook, pull up a loop and pull through the loop on the hook to make a ring. Instructions for all the flowers can be found in the patterns pages.

2. To make the first round of all of the flowers, chain 3, which counts as the first half-double crochet (hdc) and chain 1; continue to work (1 hdc and chain 1) 11 times. You will have 12 hdc and 12 chain-1 spaces. Join the round by working a slip stitch into the 2nd chain of the beginning chain 3. This completes flower 1.

3. For the flower used on the bag, work same as steps 1 and 2 above. To work the back post double crochet (bpdc), you hook and insert it from the back of the work to the front, as shown.

4. To continue the bpdc, insert the hook to the back of the work. Yarn over the hook as shown and complete the double crochet stitch. You can use the same color as the first two rounds or a different color, as used here.

5. The final round of this flower is worked in the same way as the last round of flower 2 (shown top right), but it is worked into the chain-1 spaces from round 1, as shown here.

One can never have enough jewelry, or yarn, for that matter, so this piece is the perfect combination. It's a work of wearable art.

## materials

1 ball each in #158 Buttercup (A), #103 Coral (B), #148 Turquoise (C), #194 Lime (D), and #143 Lilac (E) of Microspun by Lion Brand, 2½oz/70g balls, each approx 168yd/154m (microfiber acrylic)

Size D/3 (3.25mm) crochet hook OR SIZE TO OBTAIN GAUGE

Size 14 (.75mm) steel crochet hook for beading

Twenty-three ⅝"/16mm Luxite "Bone Rings" by Susan Bates

Forty 6mm to 10mm round glass beads

Two 10x13mm oblong glass beads

One 4mm glass bead

Sewing needle

Lime green sewing thread

## finished measurements

**The heart** Approx 3½"/9cm wide

**The chain** Approx 23½"/59.5cm long (including flower connectors)

## the gauge

6 sts to 1"/2.5cm over sc using size D/3 (3.25 mm) crochet hook. BE SURE TO GET THE GAUGE.

## how to pick up a bead

Remove loop from hook. Pick up a 6mm to 10mm bead with smaller hook, then slide bead up shaft of hook. Place loop on smaller hook and slide bead down loop. Transfer loop from smaller hook to larger hook.

## make the hearts

■ With larger hook, join A with a sl st over a bone ring. **Rnd 1 (RS)** Ch 1, work 12 sc over ring, join rnd with a sl st in first sc. Fasten off. **Rnd 2** With RS facing, join B with a sl st in any st of rnd 1. Ch 4, in 4th ch from hook work [yo and draw up a loop, yo, draw through 2 loops on hook] 4 times, yo and draw through all 5 loops on hook (petal made), ch 5, skip next st, hdc in next st, ch 3, skip next 2 sts, sc in next st, ch 4, sl st in same st as last sc, ch 3, skip next 2 sts, hdc in next st, ch 9, make another petal in 4th ch from hook, skip next st, sl st in next st leaving last st at top of heart unworked. Fasten off.

**Rnd 3** With RS facing, join C with a sl st in unworked st between petals. Ch 7, sc in top of petal, ch 7, sc in hdc, ch 4, sc in ch-4 lp, ch 4, sc in hdc, ch 7, sc in top of petal, ch 7, join rnd with a sl st in same sc as joining. **Rnd 4** Sl sl in first 3 ch of ch-7, sc in next 2 ch, hdc in next ch, work 2 hdc in last ch, dc in next sc, ch 5, sl st in top of dc just made, dc in next ch, work 2 hdc in next ch, hdc in next ch, sc in next 4 ch, sc in next sc, ch 5, sc in next sc, ch 5, sl st in 5th ch from hook (picot made), ch 5, sc in next sc, sc in next 4 ch, hdc in next ch, work 2 hdc in next ch, dc in next ch, dc in sc, ch 5, sl st in top of dc just made, work 2 hdc in next ch, hdc in next ch, sc in next 2 ch, sl st last 3 ch, join with a sl st in first sl st. Fasten off. Make 1 more heart.

## join the hearts

■ Place one heart on top of the other so WS are facing. With larger hook, join D with a sl st through both ch-5 loops at upper left heart, sc through both ch-5 loops, ch 11, sc in same ch 5-loops, ch 3, working through back loops of top heart tog with front loops of bottom heart, cont to work as folls: sc in next 9 sts, ch 6, in both ch-4 picots, work (sc, hdc, ch 5, hdc, sc), ch 6, sc in next sc, sc in next 8 sts, ch 3, in both ch-5 loops work (sc, ch 11, sc). Fasten off.

## make the chain

■ **Outer half**. With larger hook, join C with a sl st over a bone ring. Work 9 sc over ring, pick up a bead, ch 1, [work 9 sc over next bone ring, pick up a bead, ch 1] 13 times, end work 9 sc over last bone ring. Fasten off.

■ **Inner half.** With RS facing and larger hook, join D with a sl st in last st of outer half, ch 1, work 9 sc over ring, pick up a bead, ch 1, [work 9 sc over next bone ring, pick up a bead, ch 1] 13 times, end work 9 sc over last bone ring, join with a sl st in first st of outer half. Fasten off.

## make the flower connectors

■ With larger hook, join A with a sl st over a bone ring. **Rnd 1 (RS)** Ch 1, work 12 sc over ring, join rnd with a sl st in first sc. Fasten off. **Rnd 2** With RS facing, join E with a sl st in any st of rnd 1, *ch 3, pick up a bead, ch 3, skip next st, sc in next st, rep from * once more, ch 3, pick up a bead, sl st in ch-1 loop of chain, ch 3, skip next st, sc in next st, rep from * to * twice more, ch 3, pick up a bead, sl st in ch-11 loop of heart, ch 3, join rnd with a sl st in same st as joining. Fasten off. Make 1 more flower connector and connect it to opposite end of chain and ch-11 loop of heart.

## finish the necklace

■ Using a double strand of thread in sewing needle, secure end of thread to bottom of ch-5 lp at bottom tip of heart, thread on both oblong glass beads, then the 4mm bead. Insert needle back through oblong beads, then pull on thread to remove any slack. Fasten thread securely to bottom ch-5 lp.

While you can crochet away in solitude if you like, there comes a point where a little meeting of yarns, stitches and pieces must happen.

You've got your crochet full on, cruising along with no worries when suddenly you realize you are about to run out of yarn. What's a girl (or crafty guy) to do? Well, dear friends, it is time to learn the joys of joining yarn.

As with knitting, you'll want to join your yarn at the end of a row—especially if you are working

## Joining at the end of a row

To join a new ball of yarn at the side edge, tie it loosely around the old yarn, leaving at least a 6"/15cm tail. Untie the knot later and weave the ends into the seam (see "Hide and Chic" later in this chapter).

# Tie One On

an openwork or lace stitch where there's no way to weave in the ends invisibly. You may lose some yarn from the previous ball, but you can always use that for seaming fringe or tassels. Here's how it works:

## Joining yarn midrow

Before joining the new yarn midrow, complete the last stitch that you were working on. Tie the old and new together loosely close to the last stitch; yarn tails should be at least 6"/15 cm long. Later, untie the knot and weave in the ends under the stitches.

You can add some color interest to your projects by working in stripes. How best to do this depends on the stitch you are working in, but all the methods are easy enough for even a beginner to master. Let's start with **single crochet**. Ready to give it a go?

1. Work across the row until one stitch remains. Insert the hook into the last stitch and draw up a loop. Working 6"/15 cm from the end of the new color, draw the new color through both loops on the hook to complete the single crochet stitch.

drawing up the loop. Then draw the new color through all three loops on the hook to complete the stitch. Chain two and turn, then join the yarns as in Step 2, above.

For **double crochet,** you'll work until one stitch remains, then yarn over, inserting the hook into the last stitch and drawing up the loop. Next, draw the new color through the last two loops on the hook to complete the stitch. Chain three and turn, then join the yarns as in Step 2, above.

For **treble crochet,** you'll

# Stripes: Raising the Bar

2. Chain one and turn. Cut the old yarn leaving a 6"/15 cm tail. Loosely tie the two tails together, close to the side edge, so stitches don't unravel. Later, untie the knot and weave in the ends.

For **half double crochet**, you'll work until one stitch remains, then yarn over, inserting the hook into the last stitch and

work until one stitch remains. Yarn over the hook twice and draw through two loops on the hook. Yarn over again and draw through two loops on the hook. Draw the new color through the last two loops on the hook to complete the stitch. Chain four and turn, then join the yarns as in Step 2, above.

We'll show you how nice this all looks with the projects at the end of the chapter.

When you join a new ball of yarn or change colors, you'll be left with lots of loose ends. To keep your project from looking scraggly, you will have to weave in those ends. It's a tedious but necessary job. We suggest plugging into your MP3 player or parking yourself in front of the tube to ease the boredom. For threads left hanging at the sides of the work, untie any knots you made when joining the yarn and thread one loose strand into a yarn needle. Insert the needle down through the side edge for about 1½ inches, then snip off the excess. Thread the remaining strand through the

Once all pieces for your project are complete, you are ready to start putting the whole thing together. Before you begin, you'll need to pin and/or steam your pieces into shape by a process those in the needlework know call blocking. The process for crocheted pieces is the same as for knits, so flip back to page 97 to get the scoop on doing it right. (**Note:** We've said it before and we'll say it again. Blocking is a step you should never skip. So when we say go back and read all about it, we mean it.) The order in which you put your pieces together also matters. Follow the steps

# Hide and Chic:
## Weaving In Ends

needle and weave it up in opposite direction. If you changed yarns mid-row, push the knot to the wrong side of the fabric (if it isn't there already). Carefully untie the knot, thread one end of the yarn on a yarn needle and weave the needle horizontally to the right for about three stitches (check on the right side to make sure the weave isn't showing through). Pull the needle through, then take one small backstitch to secure the yarn. Snip off the excess. Do the same for the remaining loose end, weaving it to left this time.

described on page 98 of the knitting section to get it right.

Got all that done? Now you can move on to seaming the pieces together. This can be done by sewing, weaving or crocheting them to one another. Your pattern instructions may specify a certain method; if not, choose the one you think will suit the project best. Here are a few of our favorites:

# Seams
# Straightforward

## Woven seam

1. This method forms an invisible seam with no bulk. Work on a flat surface. With the right sides of both pieces facing you and the two edges adjoined, secure with safety pins every 2"/5cm. Thread a yarn needle with the tail from the foundation chain. To join the edges together before weaving, insert the needle from back to front into the corner stitch of the piece without the tail. Making a figure eight with the yarn, insert the needle, from back to front, into the stitch with the tail. Tighten to close the gap.

2. To begin weaving the seam, insert the needle through the first stitch on the left edge and then through the first stitch on the right edge. Insert the needle through the next stitch on the left edge and then through the next stitch on the right edge. Continue to alternate weaving from edge to edge in this manner, carefully matching stitches (or rows), and drawing the yarn only tight enough to keep the edges together.

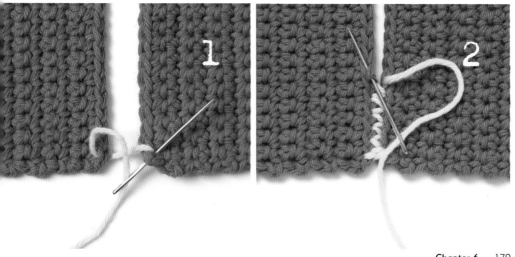

## Backstitch seam

1. The backstitch is used to create an extra-strong seam where bulk is not an issue. Place the pieces together so the right sides are facing, then pin every 2"/5cm. Thread the tail from the foundation chain into the yarn needle. Working from back to front, secure the beginning of the seam by taking the needle twice around the bottom edges. Working from back to front again, insert the needle so it exits about ¼"/5mm from the last stitch, as shown.

2. Insert the needle into the same hole as the last stitch, then back up approximately ¼"/5mm in front of the last stitch. Draw the yarn through, then tighten only enough to keep the edges together. Continue to work in this manner, taking care to keep the stitches straight and consistent in length.

## Whipstitch seam

The whipstitch is used for joining together squares like grannies for an afghan as well as other short straight edges. Thread the tail from the foundation chain in a yarn needle. Place the pieces together so the wrong side sides are facing, edges are even and stitches line up. Insert the needle into the back loop of the piece in front and into the front loop of the adjacent stitch of the piece in back. Continue to work in this manner, drawing the yarn only tightly enough the keep the edges together.

## Single crochet seam

1. Use this method for decorative exterior seams. Working from the ball of yarn, make a slip knot 6"/15cm from the yarn end. Place the slip knot on the hook. To work across top edges, place the pieces together so wrong sides are facing. Working from front to back, insert the crochet hook through both loops of each piece and draw through a loop. Yarn over and draw through both loops on hook.

Continue to work one single crochet in each pair of adjacent loops across pieces.

2. To work across side edges, place the pieces together so wrong sides are facing. Working through both thicknesses, work single crochet stitches directly into matching stitches at the side edge, making sure to space them evenly and at the same depth so that all single crochet stitches are the same size.

## Slip stitch seam

Use this technique when you want an especially sturdy join and don't mind some extra bulk. Place the pieces together right sides facing and edges even; pin every 2"/5cm. Working through both thicknesses and from front to back, insert the crochet hook between first two stitches, one stitch in from the edge. Working from the ball of yarn, catch the yarn on the wrong side (about 6"/15cm from the end) and draw through a loop. *Insert the hook between the next two stitches. Draw through a loop, then draw through the loop on the hook. Repeat from the *, keeping an even tension on the yarn so the stitches are consistent in

size and the joining has the same stretchiness as the crocheted fabric.

An entire checkers set, complete with game pieces, board and drawstring carrying bag-who'd have thought it possible? Well, you can, using the simplest crochet stitches and felting the final product for a smooth result.

## materials

2 balls each in #140 Rose (A) and #153 Ebony (B) of Lion Wool by Lion Brand, 3oz/85g balls, each approx 158yd/144m (wool)
Size K/10½ (6.5mm) crochet hook OR SIZE TO OBTAIN GAUGE

## finished measurements

### The board

Approx 19"/48cm square (after felting)

### The checkers

Approx 1¾"/4.5cm diameter (after felting)

### The bag

Approx 3½"/9cm diameter and 8½"/21.5cm high (after felting)

## the gauge

12 sts to 4"/10cm over sc using size K/10½ (6.5mm) crochet hook (before felting). BE SURE TO GET THE GAUGE.

## make the board

**Note** When changing colors, draw new color through 2 lps on hook to complete last sc.
Make 8 strips. With A, ch 8. **Row 1** Sc in 2nd ch from hook and in ch across—7 sts. Ch 1, turn. **Rows 2–7** Skip first st, sc in next 6 sts, sc in top of ch-1 t-ch of row below—7 sts. Ch 1, turn. **Row 8** Skip first st, sc in next 6 sts, sc in top of ch-1 t-ch of row below changing to B—7 sts. Ch 1, turn. Rep row 2 seven times, then rep row 8 once changing to A. Cont to work in this manner until 8 blocks have been completed.
Fasten off.

## finish the board

Sew strips tog, alternating directions and lining up intersections to achieve the checkerboard pat.

## make the border

With RS facing, join A with a sl st in any corner. **Rnd 1** Ch 1, *work 3 sc in corner, [work 8 sc along edge of next square] 8 times; rep from * around, 3 times more, ending last rep with 7 sc along edge of last square, join rnd with a sl st in first sc. **Rnds 2–3** Ch 1, sc in each st around, working 3 sc in each corner st, join rnd with a sl st in first sc. **Rnd 4** Rep rnd 2, joining rnd with a sl st in first sc changing to B. Rep rnd 2 4 times more. Fasten off.

## make the checkers

With A, ch 2. **Rnd 1** Work 8 sc in 2nd ch from hook, join rnd with a sl st in first sc. **Rnd 2** Ch 3, work 2 dc in each st around, join rnd with a sl st in 3rd ch of beg ch-3. Fasten off. Make 11 more using A and 12 using B.

## make the bag

With B, ch 2. **Rnd 1** Work 9 sc in 2nd ch from hook, join rnd with a sl st in first sc. **Rnd 2** Ch 1, work 2 sc in each st around, join rnd with a sl st in first sc—18 sts. **Rnd 3** Ch 3, [work 2 dc in next st, dc in next st] 9 times, join rnd with a sl st in 3rd ch of beg ch-3—27 sts. **Rnd 4** Ch 3, [work 2 dc in next st, dc in next 2 sts] 9 times, join rnd with a sl st in 3rd ch of beg ch-3—36 sts. **Rnd 5** Ch 3, [work 2 dc in next st, dc in next 3 sts] 9 times, join rnd with a sl st in 3rd ch of beg ch-3—45 sts. **Rnd 6** [Ch 7, skip next 5 sts, sc in next st] 7 times. **Rnds 7–9** [Ch 7, sc in next ch-7 sp] 7 times. **Rnd 10** Rep rnd 7 changing to A. **Rnds 11–14** Rep rnd 7. **Rnd 15** [Ch 7, sc in next ch-7 sp] 6 times, ch 7, join rnd with a sl st in 4th ch of next ch-7 sp. Fasten off.

## make the drawstring

With 2 strands of B held tog, make a ch 18"/45.5cm. Fasten off.

## felt the pieces

Fill washing machine to low water setting at a hot temperature. Add ¼ cup of a gentle detergent and 2 Tbs. of baking soda. Place checkers and drawstring in a zippered pillowcase cover. Place in washer the pillowcase cover, board, bag and also a pair of jeans to provide abrasion and balanced agitation. Use 15–20 minute wash cycle, including cold rinse and spin. Check measurements of pieces. If they are still bigger than finished measurements, repeat process with progressively shorter cycles, measuring every few minutes until measurements are achieved. Air-dry or machine-dry on a low setting. Steam-block to finished measurements.

## finish the bag

Weave drawstring around last rnd of B; knot ends tog.

Crown, welt and brim are worked in one piece in this charming porkpie hat. Wear it to your next poker game and you'll fit right in!

## materials

1 ball each in #158 Banana, #110 Navy, and #181 Sage of Lion Cotton by Lion Brand, 5oz/140g balls, each approx 236yd/212m(100% cotton)

Size G/6 (4mm) crochet hook OR SIZE TO OBTAIN GAUGE

An old CD and one button approx ¾"/2cm in diameter.

## the measurements

Circumference 22"/50cm

## the gauge

17 sc and 16 rnds to 4"/10cm over sc pat using size G/H (4mm) crochet hook.

BE SURE TO GET THE GAUGE.

## note

■ This three-color hat is worked as one piece from the crown to the brim.

To maintain the flat shape of the crown you will need an old CD.

## make the crown

■ With Maize, ch 5, join with sl st in first ch to form ring. **Rnd 1** Work 9 sc in ring, join with sl st in first sc—9 sc. **Rnd 2** Ch 1, 1 sc in same sc as ch 1, sc in next sc, 2 sc in next sc, *sc in next 2 sc, 2 sc in next sc; rep from *, join with sl st in first sc—12 sc. **Rnd 3** Ch 1, 1 sc in same sc as ch 1, 2 sc in next sc, *sc in next sc, 2 sc in next sc; rep from *, join with sl st in first sc—18 sc. **Rnd 4** Ch 1, 1 sc in same sc as ch 1, 2 sc in next sc; *sc in next sc, 2 sc in next sc; join with sl st in first sc—27 sc. **Rnd 5** Ch 1, 1 sc in same sc as ch 1, sc in next sc, 2 sc in next sc, *sc in next 2 sc, 2 sc in next sc; rep from *, join with sl st in first sc—36 sc. **Rnd 6** Ch1, 1 sc in same sc as ch 1, 1 sc in next 2 sc, 2 sc in next sc, *sc in next 3 sc, 2 sc in next sc; join with sl st in first sc—45 sc. **Rnd 7** Ch 1, 1 sc in same sc as ch 1, 1 sc in next 3 sc, 2 sc in next sc, *sc in next 4 sc, 2 sc in next sc; rep from *, join with sl st in first sc—54 sc. **Rnd 8** Ch 1, 1 sc into same sc as ch 1, 1 sc in next 4 sc, 2 sc in next sc, *sc in next 5 sc, 2 sc in next sc; rep from *, join with sl st in first sc—63 sc. **Rnd 9** Ch 1, 1 sc into same sc as ch 1, 1 sc in next 4 sc, 2 sc in next sc, *sc in next 5 sc, 2 sc in next sc; rep from *, join with sl st in first sc—72 sc.

## make the welt

■ **Rnds 10–15** With Navy, ch 1, 1 sc into same sc as ch 1, 1 sc in next 71 sc, join with sl st in first sc made—72 sc. **Rnds 16–19** With Sage, ch 1, 1 sc into same sc as ch 1, 1 sc in next 71 sc, join with sl st in first sc—72 sc.

## make the band

■ **Rnds 20–21** With Maize, ch 1, 1 sc into same sc as ch 1, 1 sc in next 71 sc, join with sl st in first sc—72 sc. **Rnd 22** Ch 1, 1 sc into same sc as ch 1, 1 sc in next 10 sc, 2 sc in next sc, *sc in next 11 sc, 2 sc in next sc; rep from *, join with sl st in first sc—78 sc. **Rnds 23–26** Ch 1, 1 sc into same sc as ch 1, 1 sc in next 77 sc, join with sl st in first sc—78 sc. **Rnd 27** Ch 1, 1 sc into same sc as ch 1, 1 sc in next 11 sc, 2 sc in next sc, *sc in next 12 sc, 2 sc in next sc; rep from *, join with sl st in first sc—84 sc. **Rnds 28–31** Ch 1, 1 sc into same sc as ch 1, 1 sc in next 83 sc, join with sl st in first sc—84 sc. **Rnds 32–33** With Navy, ch 1, 1 sc into same sc as ch 1, 1 sc in next 83 sc, join with sl st in first sc—90 sc. **Rnds 34–37** With Sage, ch 1, 1 sc into same sc as ch 1, 1 sc in next 83 sc, join with sl st in first sc—90 sc. **Rnds 38–39** With Navy, ch 1, 1 sc into same sc as ch 1, 1 sc in next 83 sc, join with 1 sl st in first sc—90 sc. **Rnd 40** With Maize, ch 1, 1 sc into same sc as ch 1, 1 sc in next 13 sc, 2 sc in next sc, *sc in next 14 sc, 2 sc in next sc; rep from *, join with sl st in first sc—96 sc. **Rnd 41** Ch 1, 1 sc into same sc as ch 1, 1 sc in next 95 sc, join with sl st in first sc—96 sc. **Rnd 42** Ch 1, 1 sc into same sc as ch 1, 1 sc in next 6 sc, 2 sc in next sc, *sc in next 7 sc, 2 sc in next sc; rep from *, join with sl st in first sc—108 sc. **Rnd 43** Ch 1, 1 sc into same sc as ch 1, 1 sc in next 107 sc, join with sl st in first sc—108 sc. **Rnd 44** Ch 1, 1 sc into same sc as ch 1, 1 sc in next 7 sc, 2 sc in next sc, *sc in next 8 sc, 2 sc in next sc; rep from *, join with sl st in first sc—120 sc. **Rnd 45** Ch 1, 1 sc into same sc as ch 1, 1 sc in next 119 sc, join with sl st in first sc—120 sc. **Rnd 46** Ch 1, 1 sc into same sc as ch 1, 1 sc in next 8 sc, 2 sc in next sc, *sc in next 9 sc, 2 sc in next sc: rep from *, join with sl st in first sc—132 sc. **Rnd 47** Ch 1, 1 sc into same sc as ch 1, 1 sc in next 131 sc, join with sl st in first sc—132 sc. **Rnd 48** With Sage, ch 1, 1 sc into same sc as ch 1, 1 sc in next 131 sc, join with sl st in first sc—132 sc. **Rnd 49** Work rev sc (from left to right).

## finish the hat

■ Turn hat inside out and fold where green and blue meet (blue side is 2 rows longer than green side). From green side, insert hook at bottom of green edge; as you go through to blue side the hook should be two rows away from blue edge. Sl st both sides tog. Insert CD inside crown within welt. Place button in center of CD and sew in place.

While there are certainly times when the raw edge of your work will stand on its own, most patterns call for some kind of finish along the edge of your hem, cuff or collar. This can be done with the exact same yarn, a contrasting color or a completely different fiber. (So many choices, so little crocheting time!) Anyway, it's all very easy to do. Read, look and learn as we explain below.

## Crocheting across the side edge

When working vertically, crochet stitches directly into the stitches at the side edge. Make sure to space them evenly and to go into the stitches at the same depth so that all stitches are the same size. If the edging is being added in preparation for seaming (as for afghan squares), also take care to work an equal number of edge stitches on all pieces so they will match up perfectly.

## Crocheting across the bottom edge

When working across the bottom edge, work each stitch between two stitches rather than working into the bottom loops of the foundation chain. (**Note** Working through the bottom loops will add length, so only do so when directions specifically tell you to.) If you are using a yarn of a different weight, follow the same technique as described for working across the top edge.

Adding an edging to a neckline or other curved edge will take a little more concentration. The basic technique is the same, but the even distribution of stitches becomes even more critical. Here's how to mark for a perfect finish:

# Watch Those Curves

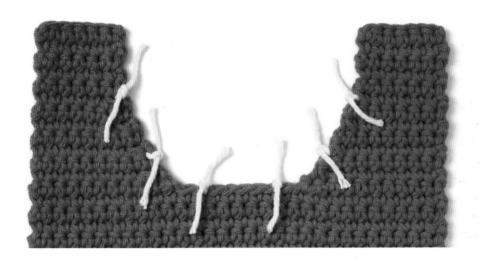

## Marking neck edge for spacing stitches

Stitches must be distributed evenly so a trim, neckband or collar will not flare out or pull in. Place pins, safety pins, or yarn markers, as shown, every 2"/5cm. If you know the number of stitches to be crocheted, divide this by the number of sections marked to determine how many stitches to work between each pair of markers. If no number is given in the directions, use the marked sections to ensure even spacing around the neck.

## tip

If you are using a thinner yarn to work your edging, you will probably need a smaller hook than the one used for your project. To get things to come out evenly, you'll need to work one stitch in some stitches and two stitches in others. If you are using a thicker yarn, you'll need to use a larger hook and work one stitch in some stitches and skip others to get it all even. You may have to rip out and start over a few times, but don't worry. With practice it'll all work out in the end.

We didn't include any crochet projects with buttonholes in this book, but you will come across them at some point. And like every good scout, we want you to be prepared for anything. So here's a quick overview of what it takes to get a buttonhole or two going.

# Who's Got the Button?

## Take two

The two-row buttonhole is the most common. It can also accommodate just about any size of button, which is a nice little perk. Here's how to work it:

1. Work to the placement of the buttonhole. Chain three (not too loosely), skip the next three stitches, then continue to work to the end of the row or to the next marker.

2. On the next row, work to the chain-three space. Work three stitches in the space, then continue to work to the end of the row or to the next chain-three space.

# Feelin' loopy

Button loops give a very femme feel to a sweater; they're also sweet on the shoulders of baby things. Here's how to make two basic styles:

## One-step button loop

Work to the placement marker of the button loop. Crochet the desired number of chain stitches (not too loosely), either don't skip any stitches or skip one or two, then continue to work to the end of the row or to the next marker.

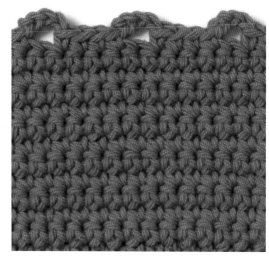

## Two-step button loop

1. Work in single crochet for about ten stitches. Chain four and turn so the wrong side is facing you. Skip two stitches, then work one slip stitch in the next stitch.

2. Chain one and turn so the right side is facing you. Work six single crochet in the loop, or as many single crochet stitches as needed to cover the loop. To continue, single crochet in the next stitch of the edge.

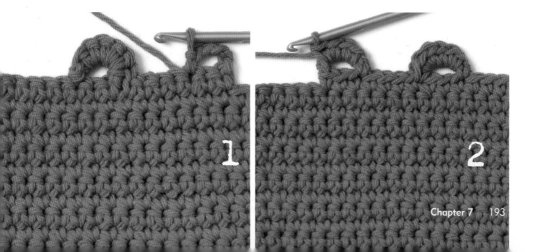

At first glance crochet instructions may seem like they're written in some sort of secret code. They're not. It's just that to save space and make directions a bit clearer, those who write patterns have come up with a few shorthand ways to get the point across. The glossary below should get you through just about any project. We've also included a handy list of U.S. crochet hook sizes and their metric equivalents.

**approx** approximately

**beg** begin, beginning

**[ ]** Repeat the directions inside the brackets as many times as indicated.

**ch** chain, chains

**cont** continue, continuing

**CC** contrasting color

**dec** decrease, decreasing

**dc** double crochet (UK: tr—treble)

**foll** follow(s), following

**hdc** half double crochet (UK: htr—half treble)

**inc** increase, increasing

**lp/lps** loop/loops

**MC** main color

**mm** millimeter, millimeters

**oz/g** ounces/grams. This usually refers to the amount of yarn in a single skein, ball or hank of yarn.

**( )** Work the directions contained inside the parentheses into the stitch indicated. See Small (Medium, Large), below, for the other uses of parentheses.

**pat/pats** pattern, patterns

**rem** remain, remains or remaining

**rep** repeat, repeating

**rep from** * Repeat the directions following the asterisk as many times as indicated. If the directions say "rep from * to end," continue to repeat the directions after the asterisk to the end of the row.

**rev sc** reverse single crochet

**reverse shaping** A term used for garments such as cardigans where shaping for the right and left fronts is identical, but reversed. For example, neck edge stitches that were decreased at the beginning of the row for the first piece will be decreased at the end of the row on the second piece. In general, follow the directions for the first piece, making sure to mirror the decreases (and/or increases) on each side.

**RS** right side, right sides

**rnd/rnds** round/rounds

**sc** single crochet (UK: dc—double crochet)

**sk** skip, skipping

**sl** slip, slipping

sl st slip st (UK: sc—single crochet)

Small (Medium, Large)
The most common method of displaying changes in a pattern for different sizes. In general, stitch counts, measurements, etc., for the smallest size come first, followed by the larger sizes in parentheses. If there is only one number given, it applies to all of the sizes.

sp space

st/sts stitch/stitches

t-ch turning chain

tog together

tr treble crochet (UK: dtr—double treble)

work even Continue in the established pattern without working any increases or decreases.

WS wrong side, wrong sides

yd/m yard(s)/meter(s)

yo yarn over

# crochet hook sizes

| U.S. | Metric | U.S. | Metric | U.S. | Metric |
|---|---|---|---|---|---|
| 14 steel | .6mm | C/2 | 2.75mm | 1/9 | 5.5mm |
| 12 steel | .75mm | D/3 | 3.25mm | J/10 | 6mm |
| 10 steel | 1mm | E/4 | 3.5mm | K/10.5 | 6.5mm |
| 6 steel | 1.5mm | F/5 | 3.75mm | L/11 | 8mm |
| 5 steel | 1.75mm | G/6 | 4mm | M/13 | 9mm |
| B/1 | 2.25mm | H/8 | 5mm | N/15 | 10mm |

# here's how

From fringe and flowers to beads and pompoms, there are all sorts of little extras you can add to your knit and crochet projects. We've included a few of our favorites here; use them as jumping-off points for you own creative flourishes.

Knit yourself a few pretty petals and watch your projects bloom!

1. For small petal, cast on 5 stitches and work 12 rows in stockinette stitch. Bind off, leaving 5"/12.5cm tails at both ends. Thread one yarn end into a tapestry needle and weave it through one long side of a knitted petal.

2. Gather the strip together to half the size and secure at the top with a backstitch. With wrong side facing out, curl one small petal as shown and tack at the bottom.

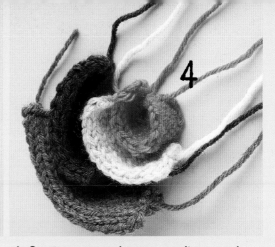

3. Overlap a second small petal around the first one and tack it at the bottom.

4. Continue to overlap two medium petals and two large petals in the same way (petals shown here have not yet been tacked in place).

# Flower Power

5. After tacking all the petals, draw all the ends to the bottom of the flower.

6. Separate the ends into two equal sections and tie them together with a triple knot. Trim the ends.

## Pompoms

Ahh, the pompom: plump, plush and ever-so-perky. Here's how to make a perfect one. You can use pompoms as a decorative trim, at the ends of cords, on hats or hoods, and for children's garments. They are easy to make.

1. With two circular pieces of cardboard the width of the desired pompom, cut a center hole. Then cut a pie-shaped wedge out of the circle. Use the templates (see Tables and Tools) as guides.

2. Hold the two circles together and wrap the yarn tightly around the cardboard. Carefully cut around the cardboard.

3. Tie a piece of yarn tightly between the two circles. Remove the cardboard and trim the pompom.

## Fringes

Fringe and tassels work up fast and fabulous. Depending on the type of yarn and where you use it, the look can be cowboy cool or showgirl sassy. We're big fans of both.

**Simple fringe** Cut yarn twice the desired length plus extra for knotting. On the wrong side, insert the hook from front to back through the piece and over the folded yarn. Pull the yarn through. Draw the ends through and tighten. Trim the yarn.

**Knotted fringe** After working a simple fringe (it should be longer to account for extra knotting), take half of the strands from each fringe and knot them with half the strands from the neighboring fringe.

**Knitted fringe** This applied fringe is worked side to side. Cast on stitches to approximately one-fifth the desired length of the fringe. Work garter stitch to the desired width of the fringe band. Bind off four to five stitches.

Unravel remaining stitches to create the fringe, which may be left looped or cut. Apply the fringe to your garment at the garter stitch border.

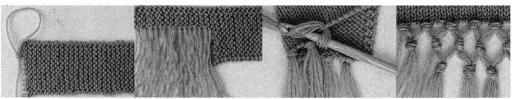

# Ends and Odds

## Tassels

**Tassel with shank** Wrap yarn around a piece of cardboard that is the desired length of the tassel. Thread a strand of yarn, insert it through the cardboard, and tie it at the top, leaving a long end to wrap around the tassel.

Cut the lower edge to free the wrapped strands. Wrap the long end of the yarn around the upper edge and insert the yarn into the top, as shown. Trim the strands.

**Tassel without shank** Wrap yarn around cardboard the length of the tassel, leaving a 12-inch (30cm) strand loose at either end. With a yarn needle, knot both sides to the first loop and run the loose strand under the wrapped strands. Pull tightly and tie at the top.

Cut the lower edge of the tassel and, holding the tassel about ¾ inch (2cm) from the top, wind the top strands (one clockwise and one counterclockwise) around the tassel. Thread the two strands and insert them through the top of the tassel.

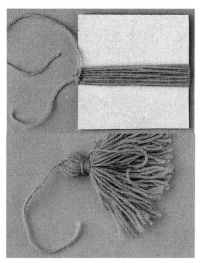

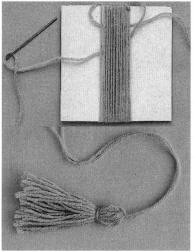

## Resources

Lion Brand Yarn Co.

34 West 15th Street

New York, NY 10011

Visit Lion Brand's website for more than 1000 knit and crochet patterns:

www.LionBrand.com

To subscribe to Knit.1 magazine, please visit www.Knit1.com.

## Designers

p. 28 Marty Miller; p. 34 Kellie Overbey; p. 36 Veronica Manno;

p. 41 Vladimir Teriokhin; p. 45 Susan Haviland; p. 47 Linda Cyr;

p. 48 Stephanie Klose; p. 50 John Brinegar; p. 54 Rebecca Rosen;

p. 56 Therese Chynoweth; p. 60 Vladimir Teriokhin; p. 64 Linda Cyr;

p. 66 Lisa Daehlin; p. 68 Tanis Gray; p. 78 Stephanie Klose; p. 80 Linda Cyr;

p. 84 Gabrielle Hamill; p. 90 Miriam Gold; p. 94 Linda Cyr;

p. 102 Linda Medina; p. 110 Joan Forgione; p. 124 Traci Bunkers;

p. 132 Marianne Forrestal; p. 134 Vladimir Teriokhin;

p. 144 Noreen Crone-Findlay; p. 146 Vladimir Teriokhin;

p. 150 Lipp Holmfeld; p. 158 Gayle Bunn; p. 162 Tanis Gray;

p. 164 Katherine Eng; p. 168 Jacqueline van Dillen;

p. 172 Noreen Crone-Findlay; p. 182 Linda Cyr; p. 186 Tony Limuaco

## Photographers

pp. 26–27, 46, 94, 95: Haitem

pp. 28, 34, 48, 50, 54, 56, 59, 80, 83, 84, 90, 93, 103, 105, 145, 162, 172, 175, 182, 184, 187, 188: Rose Callahan

pp. 36, 132, 135, 137, 147, 149, 165, 169, 171: Nick Norwood

pp. 39, 124: Jim Jordan Photography.com

pp. 40, 44, 65, 66, 78, 150, 158, 161: Paul Amato

pp. 61, 69, 110: Paul Amato for LVARepresents.com